Effectiveness and Efficiency in Higher Education for Adults

A Guide for Fostering Learning

CAEL

Council for Adult and Experiential Learning

www.cael.org

George,
Your thoughtful & insightful ideas
as an educator are
reflected in all
the ideas expressed
in this book.
Bn 2002

Your dedication
to students is
noteworthy ! at 15
your devotion
to family !
So, tired
to retire.
Love !
Cuz
Joan

KENDALL/HUNT PUBLISHING COMPANY
4050 Westmark Drive   Dubuque, Iowa 52002

Printed in the United States of America
10   9   8   7   6   5   4   3   2   1

Contents

Contents

Acknowledgements

The authors are indebted to many who have contributed in large and small ways to the development of this book. Even the long lists of references after each chapter do not exhaust the roster of those whose writings we have read in the search for what has been learned about the teaching of adults. The Reference lists identify only those from whom we have quoted or made citations on specific bodies of work.

This book was initially meant to be a second edition of *Efficiency in Adult Higher Education: A Practitioners' Handbook* (1995). Barbara Mayo-Wells, then Co-Director of the Institute for Research on Adults in Higher Education (IRAHE) and Julie Porosky, then Vice President for Continuing Education Services and University Outreach, were co-authors of that volume with Sheckley and Keeton. Much of the intellectual content of that handbook has been brought forward into the present book.

The UMUC research on which this book draws has resulted from the vision of T. Benjamin Massey, CEO of UMUC from 1978 to 1998, who initiated the formation and funding of IRAHE as President in 1990. To link the work of IRAHE with the commitment that its findings inform efforts to improve practice within UMUC, Dr. Massey created the IRAHE Coordinating Council, chaired by Dr. Porosky from 1990 through 1998. The University has, with substantial matching from its own resources, attracted major grants for IRAHE research from The Pew Charitable Trusts, an anonymous foundation, and corporate partners. Without this support the research cited herein would not have been possible.

Within UMUC every major division has contributed in some way to the IRAHE efforts. Among the most involved of the divisions, Professional Development undertook early on the case study on the nuclear physics program and more recently under Richard Dunfee and his associates managed the College-Employer Partnership Programs (CEPPs), some of which are used as application stories herein. Undergraduate Programs, the Graduate School of Management and Technology, and Student Services have served as primary arenas of inquiry in the Diverse Students Program, the Effectiveness and Efficiency in Learning Program, and some of the College-Employer Programs projects. Then Dean Paul Hamlin (UGP), then Dean Nick Allen (GSMT; now Provost and Chief Academic Officer), then Associate Dean, now Dean, Mary Ellen Hrutka (UGP), Vice President Porosky, and recently Diana Lampe (Student Services) have led these divisions during the years of IRAHE research. The EXCEL Program, directed by Theresa Hoffmann, is the primary subject of two of the studies.

After the retirement of Dr. Mayo-Wells, her successor Dr. Joan Krejci, now Griggs, joined Drs. Keeton and Sheckley as co-author of this book. With the encouragement of Dr. Krejci, the authors decided to organize the treatment of best practices around a limited set of principles rather than around the arenas of practice. The change was so substantial as to dictate treating the current book as a different animal from the earlier *Handbook*.

Throughout IRAHE's history Barry Sheckley, head of the Adult Learning Program of the Neag School of Education, University of Connecticut at Storrs, has been the lead research consultant as well as co-author of this work. He served as formative and summative evaluator of Stages 1 and 2 of the Diverse Students Program. IRAHE also contracted with him and his graduate students for selected projects and studies. The contributions provided by John Cubeta, Maryanne Legrow, Henriette Pranger, Nan Travers, and Peter Kennedy are cited directly in the chapter references. Insights provided by Professor Marijke Kehrhahn, developed from her work with student-centered research teams, have enriched the thinking of the authors in many areas. Additionally the help provided by graduate students in the Adult Learning Program, especially the many hours of assistance contributed by Sue Gregoire, accelerated the completion of the book. Finally, the authors wish to acknowledge the assistance of the Neag School of Education at the University of Connecticut through its encouragement of the research contributing to this book.

Altogether IRAHE's grants have supported more than 25 case studies of programs that have been especially effective in the use of student and faculty time and in saving costs to their institutions. The authors of the case studies are named in the master list of those studies in Appendix A.

Tom Flint, Vice President of CAEL (Council for Adult and Experiential Learning) and head of CAEL Publications, read an early full draft of the book and offered helpful counsel. As the manuscript reached penultimate draft, we asked Professor Wilbert McKeachie of the University of Michigan to critique the text. His detailed comments have been most helpful in making sure that the best of research on college teaching has been reflected in the manuscript. In addition, Dr. Margaret Chambers, head of the Institute for Distance Education in the Office of Distance Education and Lifelong Learning (ODELL) has done a similar review and added suggestions adopted by the authors. Norman Evans of Goldsmith's College, The University of London, and long-time colleague in scholars exchanges and in the fostering of assessment services on prior experiential learning, also carried out a reading of the manuscript and made suggestions that we have incorporated into the final text. Dr. Morry Fiddler of the School for New Learning, DePaul University, has read and contributed ideas for a number of chapters as they neared final form. Professor Irwin Abrams and Archivist Scott Sanders of the Antioch University Archives unearthed needed articles by Alexander Astin that documented Antioch College's educational productivity.

In the IRAHE Office staff support was provided by Eugenia Moreno in the early years and in the late, most demanding phases, by Linda Olson, Administrative

Assistant. Sarah Doran, a senior majoring in history at University of Maryland College Park helped with documentation of references. Joan Keeton Young, General Assistant to Morris Keeton, has done troubleshooting and support for his work throughout.

As the book goes to press, we owe special thanks to CAEL for its sponsorship and services in promoting its members' use of this book.

The authors would like to thank their families and friends for their many contributions to our work. Their support has occurred many times in behind-the-scenes efforts that enabled the authors to devote time and energy to the writing when other issues clamored for attention.

The Authors

May, 2002

Preface

Fostering Effective and Efficient Learning by Adults

Early in 1996 a major telecommunications company invited University of Maryland University College (UMUC) to bid on a contract to update a series of cohorts of "legacy programmers" of 18-20 members per cohort. The company spelled out in detail the skills that the trainees should acquire and proposed a 26-week schedule using the latest computer equipment. The goal was proficiency in applying the latest languages, hardware, and software in telecommunications. The instruction would occur in the company's worksite. To facilitate the University's service the company provided the instructors with the same equipment its employees would use. The company wanted the trainees not only to use new programming languages with state-of-the-art hardware (smart terminals with a networking server rather than dumb terminals with a larger central computer), but also to learn how to adapt as further changes in hardware and software would occur.

During the next two years, the training period was shortened for some cohorts, the curriculum content was adapted each time for each cohort, more than one worksite came to be used, and one cohort was taught onsite at the university headquarters. Rapid adjustment to the specific needs of each cohort and of the changing company situation was required with each cohort to reach the level of effectiveness sought.

This project proved to be highly efficient for the employees, the company, and the university. For the employees there was no tuition cost—the company paid all. Employees also saved study time and commuting time: all classes were provided at their usual worksite except for one cohort, and half of class hours were on paid work time for all cohorts. Between classes the students could interact with instructors online. For employee-students with young children, the child care costs were sharply reduced. Commuting costs for workers in most cohorts were eliminated. The trainees were assured of continuing employability that they would not otherwise have enjoyed.

For the company the efficiency derived from its having put the contract out to competitive bidding. Also the risks and costs of recruiting new workers in a short-supply labor market were avoided. For the university savings resulted from the company's use of its own worksite (UMUC normally rented classroom space for such classes from an adjacent university) and from the company's giving state-of-the-art computers for instructor use and for ongoing university ownership.

This story, along with others in this book, reflects an emerging pattern of more efficient and effective educational services colleges are providing—services that enable adult learners to reach new levels of proficiency as job requirements change. This case illustrates how educational services can be tailored to meet employees' specific situations, to help them become effective lifelong learners, minimizing unnecessary costs to them and to their employers, evaluated at each stage of the provision of service, and rapidly revised on the basis of that evaluation to sustain the effectiveness and efficiency of the effort. (Keeton, Mayo-Wells, et. al, 1999). The program, similar to others reviewed in this book, is designed for learners to achieve proficiency, an end goal that represents having knowledge as well as having competence in applying the knowledge skillfully.

TO WHOM IS THIS BOOK ADDRESSED?

This book is addressed to educators who want to respond effectively to needs such as this story exemplifies. The book is for those who want to help adult learners in colleges or universities learn better with less time and cost. These educators may be instructors, program chairs, department heads, student support personnel, information technology specialists, academic deans, or other administrators. Not all educators want to devote their own time to enhancing the efficiency as well as the effectiveness of their work, but most will welcome its being done in the interest of broader access, affordability, and success for students. As growing numbers of working adults return to college and to graduate and professional study to meet the changing skill and knowledge demands of work settings, it is basic to economic health, good citizenship, and societal well-being to make the learning effort both more efficient and more effective. For this reason we, the authors, group the chapters of this book so that readers can focus on options most relevant to their own roles.

DIFFICULTIES WITH IMPROVING EFFECTIVENESS AND EFFICIENCY IN LEARNING

A number of difficulties confront educators who want to enhance adults' learning, notably the complexity of the art and the demands of the different modes of instruction, of the various roles for teachers, and of the interests among students. The complications are further magnified by our limited knowledge about the best ways to elicit learning when these complexities all interact in one setting.

The central difficulty is that facilitating learning is an art and a difficult one at best. An art is more than a matter of knowledge: it involves also skill, understanding, and practice. Understanding occurs best when individuals grasp principles that research has found basic to best practice. Using this understanding artfully, however, requires both skill and practice in the implementation of the principles and judgment as to where and how they are applicable.

A next difficulty derives from the fact that applying principles artfully requires the use of both strategies and tactics. Knowing the principles but not the strategies may yield theoretical understanding that does not translate into effective practice. Having the tactics of a good practitioner without mastery of relevant principles can lead to a poor choice of strategy and a poor instructional design. In addition, principles, strategies and tactics often are used in combinations. In a concrete situation such as all instruction and learning involve, effective instructors cannot act on only one principle of learning at a time: unavoidably more than one principle or strategy is involved, and sometimes these principles and strategies may seem to conflict with one another in the procedures demanded.

Facilitating learning calls for strategies that differ as the requirements of discrete situations call for distinct modes of instruction. This difficulty becomes even more complex with online studies. Teachers working online face different opportunities, have different tools with which to work, and face different obstacles to success than do their colleagues teaching in face-to-face classrooms.

The complexity of providing educational services to different learners in unique settings also compounds the difficulties student support personnel face in providing effective help for learners. Student support professionals can work with learners' self-confidence, their help-seeking habits, and their coping with obstacles—matters that an instructor also could address—but at costs in time that may be prohibitive. Some problems in making learning efficient can best be approached at a program design level. Changes made at this broader level can introduce innovations with a much wider scope than those introduced at the level of individual courses. Commitments from the leadership of academic and administrative authorities are also necessary to create conditions at an institutional level that are conducive to learning; e.g., seeing that all students have ready access to computers, ready access to the Internet, and convenient access to instruction. In addition, effectiveness and efficiency in learning require an institutional culture that encourages and supports career and intellectual development over fun-seeking and self-indulgence.

Since learners do not all have the same interests, backgrounds, and goals, they require different kinds of support. Learners differ in their levels of preparation for college or graduate school, in their learning styles, in the cultures to which they are native, in their levels of confidence in themselves as learners, in the stresses and responsibilities they bear while engaged in study, and in their financial and other resources for learning. Institutions of postsecondary education increasingly bear responsibility for tailoring their services to the distinctive needs and capabilities of their students. We focus in some of this book's chapters on the accommodations being made to these conditions.

How This Book Helps Educators

To help readers cope with the difficulties and the complexity of the task they face, we have begun with an overview of key principles for enhancing learning and ways in which these principles may be applied. In the ensuing chapters we deal in detail with strategies for employing the principles, present stories about ways the strategies have been successfully used, and reference the research that has led to our adoption of the principles. In each of these chapters we address the application of the principles in activities at different levels (classroom, online, program, and institution).

To master the art of developing and using knowledge well, Alfred North Whitehead (1929) suggested that learners must move up and down "the abstraction ladder." Learners might first move from principle to specific case. Knowing specifics of a certain case, they would then move back up the ladder to explore the strategy and the principle with questions and further reflection. With this new understanding in hand, they would then move down again to the arena of practice to try a different strategy. This book is designed to follow this kind of instructive movement up and down the abstraction ladder. By exploring specific stories and cases, the discussions presented throughout the book highlight the interplay of principles and strategies that have served to enhance effectiveness and efficiency in learning in a wide range of diverse situations.

What Is Distinctive about This Book?

What then is distinctive about this book? It is not its articulation of new principles. Since the principles are based on existing research, they cannot be new: they represent instead a careful integration of ideas educators may find useful for enhancing the learning of adult students.

Nor is the book's distinctiveness a matter of nominating novel tactics. While relatively novel tactics may be emerging with the development of new communications technologies, most of their applications have in some form been tried and tested before. There are books with tips on good practice in the more familiar arenas of postsecondary education, notably McKeachie's *Tips on Teaching* (1994) in its numerous editions.

The novelty of our book, we believe, is in its bringing together these current resources in the interest of *efficiency* for the learner, for the institution, and for those who pay the tuition and taxes that further access. The "efficiency" sought is not one of lowering the cost per credit hour or degree award for attendance in college. That kind of cost containment can occur *at the expense of more effective learning* and of more cost-effective use of faculty talent. Our focus calls for seeing all of the elements of effective facilitation of learning and for understanding how they interact and can be tried in different settings in the search for improvement in the amount of learning, in its depth and complexity (as in higher order thinking skills), and in its retrieval and application when needed. Those who use this book as intended will be co-investigators of a developing art of achieving such efficiency.

Even today higher education at the undergraduate level tends to emphasize the mastery of narrative knowledge (information and theory) to the neglect of the development of proficiency—the skilled use of knowledge in practice. This book proposes ways to avoid this mistake.

A less obvious distinction of this book is its attention to relatively new insights into the nature of learning and problem-solving. One of these insights has to do with the nature and roles of implicit learning in the development of expertise of all kinds, including expertise as learners (Reber, 1993). Another insight arises from recognizing the variety of ways in which diversity of cultures affects what can be learned and alters the supports needed by different learners (Diouf, Sheckley, Kehrhahn, 2000). Still another insight relates to the ways in which "communities" of learners can affect their learning (Schneider, 1991). These new areas of insight are of particular significance in the educational community's growing effort to improve instruction with the help of emerging communications technologies.

We begin in Chapter 1 of this book with a story and an overview of principles of instruction. Thereafter we offer a story to begin each chapter and follow with a statement of the principle to be highlighted in that chapter. Principles embody the theory by which we organize our understanding of human experience. Stories of their application embody the confusing complexity of reality that can never be fully captured by theory. The expert educator draws upon both to engage in a career-long drive toward efficiency in learning.

REFERENCES

Diouf, W., Sheckley, B., & Kehrhahn, M. (2000). Adult learning in a non-western context: The influence of culture in a Senegalese farming village. *Adult Education Quarterly, 51:*(1) 32-44.

Keeton, M. T.; Mayo-Wells, B.; Porosky, J. E.; and Sheckley, B. G. (1999). *Efficiency in Adult Higher Education: A Practitioners Handbook.* Adelphi, MD: Institute for Research on Assessment in Higher Education, University of Maryland University College.

McKeachie, W. J., Cham N., Menges, R., Svinicki, M. & Weinstein, C. E. (1994). *Teaching tips: Strategies, research, and theory for college and university teachers. Ninth Edition.* Lexington, MA: Heath & Company.

Reber, A. S. (1993). Implicit learning and tacit knowledge: An essay on the cognitive unconscious. New York: Oxford University Press.

Schneider, D. J. (1991). Social cognition. *Annual Review of Psychology, 42,* 527-561.

Whitehead, A. N. (1929). *Process and reality.* New York: The Macmillan Company.

CHAPTER 1

Achieving Efficiency in Learning

An Overview of Research-Based Principles

Higher education in the United States is under attack as never before for its alleged failure to prepare graduates with the thinking, writing, and other skills that tuition payers, taxpayers, and others have funded it to provide. The attackers argue that the time of faculty is not being appropriately used for the purposes for which this support has been given. These and related demands for increased accountability, improvements in "quality," and advances in efficiency have recently grown more widespread and insistent than before (Harvey & Knight, 1996).

Models of effective and efficient teaching at course level, at program level, and institution-wide that exist among U. S. universities and colleges can address these calls for reform. This book argues that efficiency and accountability in higher education can be achieved in reasonable measure if a set of key principles is applied. The principles, of course, must be applied by appropriate strategies and imaginative use of technology.

In this opening chapter we provide an overview of a set of principles to achieve effectiveness and efficiency in learning. In the chapters that follow we discuss their application. Using our own version of Occam's razor (i.e., we assume no entities beyond necessity), we present only eight principles. This parsimonious choice, we hope, will permit a clear statement of the principles, of cases that illustrate their application, and of the research on which they are based. We believe also that educators who use the principles will find applying just eight principles a more manageable task than dealing with a larger set. The eight principles are based on research that suggests that their use will account for learning gains of the largest size. This research is drawn from a wide range of fields including cognitive psychology, neurophysiology, anthropology, and teacher education. As the discussion will illustrate, the principles apply to learning at work, in college, in distance education, through community activities, as well as in self-directed activities. The principles apply to learners of all kinds.

The rising numbers of working adult learners who are now participating in postsecondary education prompt us to give special attention to these older learners who

1

represent a relatively new population in higher education [NCES, 1996]. Our hope is that the book will help teachers teach older learners more effectively. We also anticipate that this volume will help administrators understand better how they can foster teaching effectiveness and provide an efficient context for it.

Gaining Proficiency: A First Story about Research on Principles: The General and the Surgeon

Proficiency—the ability to use skillfully an amalgam of knowledge and competence—is the goal of learning. How can it best be reached? A story from the annals of research will clarify the goal and some of the complexities of reaching it.

Two researchers (Gick & Holyoak, 1983) created a set of experiments to learn more about how individuals learn. In Part 1 of their study a first group of learners (the control group, getting no special assistance) were asked to solve the following problem:

As a medical doctor you are treating a patient afflicted with a malignant tumor in his stomach. If you do not remove the tumor, the patient will die soon. You have at your disposal a laser ray that can destroy the tumor. Unfortunately the intensity of the ray required to destroy the tumor will also destroy all healthy tissue in its path. If you lowered the intensity of the ray to a certain level, you could shoot it into the body without harming any healthy tissue. This lower density, however, would not eliminate the tumor. Can you save the patient?

As shown in Figure 1-1, only 10% of the participants in this control group figured out that the laser beam could be broken into a cluster of laser beams in which each was of an intensity that would not harm healthy tissue. If all these lower intensity rays in the cluster could, from different sources and directions, be focused and shot into the body so that they would arrive simultaneously at the tumor, they could eradicate the tumor without harming other tissues.

In Part 2 of the experiment, the participants were either: (a) told a story about how a similar problem was solved, (b) told an abstract principle that could be used to solve the problem, or (c) shown a diagram of a strategy that could be used to solve the problem. The participants were then given the original problem. Notice that the success rates in conditions (a) and (b) almost tripled—from 10% to 30%—though the large majority of participants (70%) still did not solve the problem.

In Part 3 of the experiment, participants were again: (a) told a story about how a similar problem was solved, (b) told an abstract principle that could be used

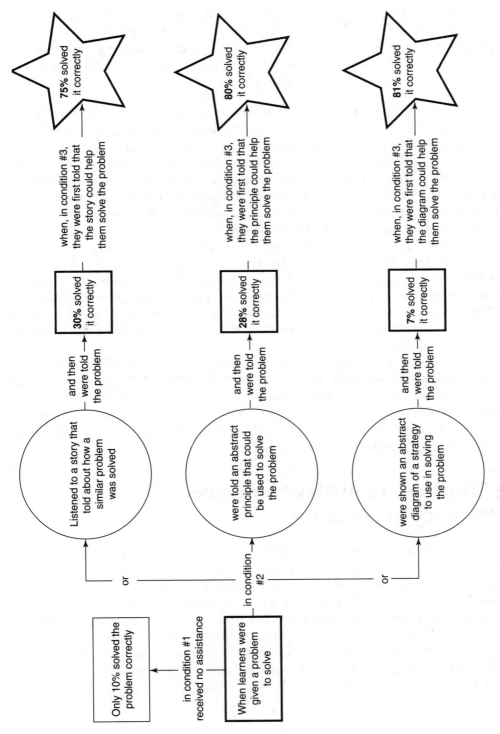

Figure 1-1. Gick, M. and Holyoak, K. (1983). Schema induction and analogical transfer. *Cognitive Psychology, 15,* 1-38.

*to solve the problem, or (c) shown a diagram of a strategy that could be used to solve the problem. But this time, before being given the medical problem to solve, the participants were told that the story, principle, or diagram was a **hint** that could be used to solve the medical problem. Notice that the success rate jumped almost 800% from that in the initial situation.*

What does this experiment have to do with improving efficiency in learning? In Part 1 of the study the learners were clearly not proficient in solving the problem. To assist them, their instructors (the experimenters) provided in Part 2 the knowledge that individuals would need to solve the problem. The results indicated that most of the learners (70%) were still not proficient enough to apply the knowledge skillfully to the problem at hand. Only when the experimenters provided an additional instructional support in the form of a hint was a plurality of the participants able to use the information at hand to solve the problem.

All the learners in Part 2 had acquired the knowledge necessary to solve the problem. The fact that they did not use this knowledge to solve the problem makes clear that knowledge alone does not guarantee proficiency and suggests that instructional strategies that strive only to help learners acquire knowledge will fall short of helping them develop the intended proficiency. The hint turned out to be a critical instructional support that enabled the participants to use the knowledge at hand to solve the problem skillfully.

This result suggests that instructional strategies will be successful to the extent that they provide explicit supports to help learners understand the link between the information provided and how that information can be used skillfully. The strategies outlined in this volume provide specific guidance on ways to provide such instructional supports. For instance, the use of genuine problems in furthering knowledge improves the chances of achieving proficiency as well.

Using Principles to Achieve Effectiveness and Efficiency in Learning

How can we use principles well, gaining their advantages and minimizing their limitations? A clue is embedded in a saying about novices and experts: "A novice," the saying goes, "follows rules. An expert is guided by stories."

Novices have had very little experience in their work as compared with experts (Ericsson & Lehmann, 1996) and thus know less about mistakes to avoid and diverse routes to success (Miller & Perlis, 1997). They are less skilled in sizing up situations (Endsley, 1997). They tend to go at once to trial and error in seeking solutions. Experts, by contrast, tend before acting to review and weigh advantages of different ways they have dealt with a situation. Novice clinicians, for instance, have seen fewer different manifestations of a given illness and know less of alternative diagnoses and, for each diagnosis, of alternative treatments (Chi, Glaser & Farr, 1988). Such novice clinicians tend to rely on rules provided by their supervisors. As they bring their rules into real life situations they encounter cases that call for exceptions to the rules. From these instances the novices learn to subordinate the rules to general principles. With further attempts to apply the principles in real world situations, the learners see that the principles sometimes conflict with one another in practice. Then the problem becomes one of striking a balance among rules and principles and integrating their use insightfully (Chi et al, 1988). Experts, by contrast with novices, monitor their own activities and are more likely to catch their mistakes (Weinberg, 1991). Expertise is thus an advanced level of proficiency. Experts benefit from real life applications of knowledge ("stories") they have accumulated over years of experience (Scribner, 1986).

Education is the highly complex art of giving optimal weight to principles on facilitating learning, principles that in practice seem at times to be antithetical to one another. This book is meant to help its users develop the art of striking the best balance in practice. Knowing stories about how to do so is often the best way of conveying the essence of this art—hence our having begun with the Gick and Holyoak story. In that story different learners needed different levels of support to solve the problem. A few immediately figured out how to solve the surgeon's problem, but most needed more information. Even with all of the information needed to solve the problem at hand, however, over 70% still needed further support, a hint, to move from having much information to its transformation into knowledge and from there to *proficiency* in applying it to the problem. Likewise, knowing the principles of learning alone does not suffice to make a good teacher. In Chapters 2 through 9, accordingly, the authors provide stories as examples or hints of strategies and tactics that can be used in applying the principles effectively.

COMPACTING PRINCIPLES INTO A USABLE SUMMARY

In this chapter then we list eight key principles that can be used to further effectiveness and efficiency in learning. In the ensuing chapters we spell out strategies that can be used to implement each principle. We also illustrate instances of their use. Learning is a wonderfully complex activity. For a teacher efforts to enhance it can present a baffling challenge. Add the challenge of teaching on-line, and the difficulty of the enhancing student learning is compounded.

In our grouping of principles we have emphasized especially those that research suggests are big ticket items; that is, their effects are not just statistically significant, but their use yields the largest effects among available practices in furthering the intended learning (Sheckley & Keeton, 1997b). Neither the principles listed in Table 1-1 nor the practices cited, however, are an exhaustive list.

Table 1-1. Principles for enhancing effectiveness and efficiency in learning

Principle	Practice
Principle 1: Early and ongoing clarification of goals and of a route to their achievement will facilitate learning.	Set clear goals, design a plan for reaching them, and enlist learners' commitment by a continuing review that refines and updates both goals and plans.
Principle 2: Deliberate practice in the route to the goals will enhance and deepen the learning.	Use repeated practice and supportive feedback in pursuit of the goals.
Principle 3: Balancing the challenge of high expectations with supports tailored to the individual learner's needs in meeting the challenge can yield increased learning and development.	Provide an optimal balance of challenge and support that is tailored to the individual's readiness and potential.
Principle 4: A rich body of experience is essential for optimum learning. Those who engage in direct experience of an object of study will normally learn more accurately and penetratingly about it than those who do not experience it directly.	Broaden the learners' experience of the matter being studied.
Principle 5: Experience yields explicit (narrative) knowledge only if actively reflected upon. Such reflection often occurs best in interaction with peers, instructors, or other active questioners.	Reflecting upon one's ways of reflection can yield a double benefit by enhancing a learner's power to learn. Elicit active and critical reflection by learners on their growing experience base.
Principle 6: Using genuine problems as a focal point of inquiry serves as a catalyst that optimizes the interaction between broadening experience and reflection on it.	Link inquiries to genuine problems or issues that are of high interest to the learners in order to enhance their motivation and accelerate their learning.
Principle 7: Early and continuing focus on the learners' becoming highly effective in learning can speed up and deepen learning in later work.	Develop students' effectiveness as learners early in their education.
Principle 8: For an institution to assist learners best in their learning, it must embody a pervasive climate that creates a culture of learning by encouraging and supporting searching and unfettered inquiry.	Create an environment that supports and encourages inquiry.

What Is the Evidence for the Importance of These Principles?

Our choice of principles and practices to emphasize derives from the findings of multiple lines of research, from case studies in the practice of college-level instruction for adults and in corporate employee development, and from our own experiences as students and teachers. We distinguish sharply between empirical research and anecdotal accounts about learning by, and instruction of, adults. Less rigorous methods can evoke significant hypotheses about how best to learn, but only sound empirical research seems to us to warrant recommendations for wider use.

The reference sections of this book provide a selection of readings on research regarding these eight principles. Especially important among the references are those in which a large number (25 or more, typically) of empirical studies on the same matter have been analyzed—meta-analyses. Such principles are most likely to be widely applicable. In the chapters 2 through 9 we draw on these references and discuss strategies and tactics for the effective implementation of the principles.

REFERENCES

Chi, M. T. H., Glaser, R. & Farr, M. J. (Eds.). (1988). *The nature of expertise.* Hillsdale, N.J.: Lawrence Erlbaum Associates, Publishers.

Endsley, M. R. (1997). The role of situation awareness in naturalistic decision making. In G. Zsambok & C. Klein (Ed.): *Naturalistic decision making.* Mahwah, N.J.: Lawrence Erlbaum Associates, Publishers.

Ericcson, K. A. & Lehmann, A. C. (1996). Expert and exceptional performance. Evidence of maximal adaptation to task constraints. *Annual Review of Psychology, 47,* 273-305.

Gick, M. L. & Holyoak, K. J. (1983). Schema induction and analogical transfer. *Cognitive Psychology, 15,* 1-38.

Harvey, L., & Knight, P. T. (1996). *Transforming higher education.* Buckingham, UK: The Society for Research into Higher Education & The Open University Press.

Miller, M. & Perlis, D. (1997). Toward automated expert reasoning and expert-novice communication. In P. J. F. Feltovich, K. M. Ford & R. R. Hoffman (Eds.): *Expertise in Context.* Cambridge, MA: The MIT Press.

NCES. (1996). *Nontraditional undergraduates: Trends in enrollment from 1986 to 1992 and persistence and attainment among 1989-90 beginning postsecondary students (NCES, 97-578).* Washington, DC: National Center for Educational Statistics, U.S. Department of Education.

Scribner, S. (1986). Thinking in action: Some characteristics of practical thought. In R. J. Sternberg and R. K. Wagner: *Practical intelligence: Nature and origins of competence in the everyday world.* Cambridge, MA: Cambridge University Press.

Sheckley, B. G. & Allen, G. A. (1991). Experiential learning: A key to adult development. In L. Lamdin (Ed.): *Roads to the Learning Society*. Chicago: Council for the Advancement of Adult and Experiential Learning.

Sheckley, B. G. & Keeton, M. T. (1997a). *Improving employee development: Perspectives from research and practice*. Chicago: Council for Adult and Experiential Learning.

Sheckley, B. G. & Keeton, M. T. (1997b). *A review of the research on learning: Implications for the instruction of adult learners*. Paper presented at the AAHE Planning Meeting, Denver, CO.

Sheckley, B. G. & Keeton, M. T. (1999). *Ecologies that support and enhance adult learning*. Paper presented at the International Assembly, Council for Adult and Experiential Learning, Seattle, Washington.

Weinberg, S. (1991). Historical problem solving: A study of the cognitive processes used in the evaluation of documentary and pictorial evidence. *Journal of Educational Psychology, 83:* (1) 73-87.

CHAPTER 2

Get Clear and Stay Clear
on What to Learn and How

If you were building a house, you would first anchor the footers in the bedrock and then erect the main load-bearing structures (walls and beams). Next you would fill in with interior and exterior structures and materials before the final steps of painting, polishing, and decorating.

So it is with the process of instruction—the facilitating of learning. If at the outset certain key processes are built into the "load-bearing" capability of the instructional activity, it can then expeditiously and effectively further the intended learning. This approach applies whether the learning experiences are classroom-based courses, laboratories, service-learning experiences, learning in the workplace, learning online, or learning on one's own.

The eight key processes identified in Chapter 1 as principles for facilitating learning are the load-bearing structures for use by instructors. How to apply these principles is the focus of this and the following eight chapters.

Principle 1: Get Clear on What to Learn and How

To learn most effectively and efficiently, learners should understand clearly what is to be learned and how. The goals and the ways to reach them must be clear to both instructor and students. As learning proceeds and the goals are modified, a shared understanding between instructors and learners needs to be sustained.

This principle was applied effectively in an effort in the University of Connecticut's Neag School of Education to improve the quality of dissertations and to shorten the time the average candidate would need to complete the doctorate.

A Shorter, Better Route to the Doctorate

Doctoral students, referred to in the literature as "the forgotten majority," can spend up to 11 years or more completing their Ph.D. programs (Baird, 1990; Baldwin & Thelin, 1990) The Ford Foundation spent almost a half a million dollars in the 1960s to support efforts in ten prestigious universities to shorten the average time-to-the-doctorate from 7 years to a target 5 years, but without success (Magat, 1979). Typically graduate students who have been well motivated and efficient during their coursework become very inefficient and ineffective as they move to complete their dissertation research.

In line with this research, faculty in the University of Connecticut's School of Education documented between 1985 and 1992 that students in its Adult Learning Program (ALP) were taking about 8 years to complete the requirements for a doctoral degree. The faculty concluded that the program needed to be structured so that students learned more effectively and efficiently. To do so the faculty devised more productive learning arrangements with a clear goal requiring students to complete their degrees in fewer years. (Kehrhahn, Sheckley & Travers, 2000)

In a revised first year orientation program (instituted 1992 and 1993), the University's ALP faculty set four goals: (1) preserve the program's academic quality; (2) reduce the total time for students to declare a research topic from 3 years to 1 year; (3) reduce the total time for students to have a research proposal accepted from 5 plus years to 2.5 years; and (4) reduce the total time for students to earn a degree from 7 plus years to 5 years or fewer.

Beginning in 1993 the requirement of adhering to the schedule was reinforced continually with the ALP students during core courses and research seminars by clarifying expectations of what constitutes "doctoral level work" and by setting explicit goals for completion of each stage of this work. Instructors provided structured assistance by integrating major course assignments and program activities on the one hand with specific requirements of the degree program, including steps in dissertation completion. For example, research papers and examinations during coursework were designed so that each activity advanced students one more step toward completion of their comprehensive examinations and dissertation research. In each core course, to help students master research skills needed for their dissertations, students completed research projects that involved gathering, analyzing, and summarizing data and then integrating this data within a theoretical framework. Research seminars in which students developed their research papers built upon and expanded the skills they developed in the core courses.

Students were also formed into cohorts who worked throughout the program as research teams. Faculty assisted the teams when needed. The clear new goals of the experimental program provided a strong challenge to students while simultaneously providing supports to help students meet these challenges. For example, as faculty challenged students to develop research proposals, students were supported through collaboration with cohorts in their research teams and through deliberate practice that enhanced their research skills.

Actual outcomes for the post-1993 entering groups as of 2000 were: (1) improved products (literature studies, team projects, individual research papers, dissertations); (2) mean time to accepted proposal down from 5.4 years to 2.8 years; (3) mean time *to degree down from 7.8 years to 5.6 years. In addition, faculty time and costs to the university were saved by greater mutual support among students and by greater use of group settings for faculty supports.*

Important efficiencies were realized in the new program: (1) Graduate students in the experimental group saved time by advancing in the steps of their degree program more rapidly than were those in the comparison group; (2) Students in the intervention group reported more positive feelings about their experience, less isolation, less stress, and more successes than did their counterparts. While shortening time to degree the new program increased time on task for students by saving their time on bureaucratic problems and time spent by them in unproductive or inefficient efforts. No increases in class time or faculty supports were required to achieve these gains. (Kehrhahn, Sheckley, & Travers, 2000).[1]

This story offers a plain illustration of Principle 1: Learners do best if they understand early and concur in what and how they are to learn. While this experiment yielded a clear way to improve efficiency in doctoral programs, the authors caution that "No one set of generic interventions exists that will guarantee improved efficiency of all graduate programs" (Kehrhahn, Sheckley, Travers, 2000, p. 9). Instead, the researchers suggest seven general guidelines for educators seeking to adapt the findings to their own programs:

- Define explicitly the core tasks required for completion of the degree program.
- Propose a timeline with explicit milestones for degree completion.
- Assist students in managing their academic goals.
- Provide task specific supports to help students overcome the obstacles and barriers to degree completion.
- Maximize time on tasks related directly to completion of degree requirements.
- Use fully the resources, skills, and expertise each student brings to the program.
- Develop a feedback process designed to improve continuously and refine the efficiency of the program (Kehrhahn, Sheckley, Travers, 2000, p. 8).

Proficiency in some form is typically the goal of a learning effort. Usually students enroll in a college course in order to gain information about a particular discipline (e.g., algebra, ethical theory) or skills in a specific vocation (e.g., civil engineering, personnel management). In the longer run, proficiency, the skilled use of this knowledge, is their goal.

Proficiency in any of these contexts is a fusion of being knowledgeable with being competent. All of the principles articulated in Chapter 1 can contribute to achieving the desired proficiencies. Proficiency is a compound that requires a rich experience base in the field of expertise (Principle 4), a well-developed body of

---

[1]This case illustrates many of the principles we advocate. For purposes of this chapter only Principle 1 is highlighted. References to this case will be made later in the book in discussions of other principles.

knowledge, the capacity for complex reflection on the experience and knowledge (Principle 5), and thus higher order thinking skills and habits of persistent inquiry and effective application of ideas (Principle 7).

We begin our discussion of applying Principle 1 by outlining in Table 2-1 a practical set of strategies for developing clear goals.

GETTING THE TEACHERS' GOALS CLEAR TO THE STUDENTS

In a four-year teaching experiment involving 15 instructors, the senior author received a shock at the very outset. A pretest had been given to students in each course so that its results could be compared with end-of-course results. In the senior author's course, students expressed surprise at the questions on the pretest. The instructor thought that the syllabus clearly defined the knowledge to be measured. "Not so," said the students. "The language of the syllabus is too abstract. We can't translate it into clear expectations about the test." When the instructor explained that the knowledge and skills to be assessed at the end of the course would be the same as those assessed in the pre-test, students understood what they needed to learn.

This example illustrates a key practice for implementing Principle 1. To clarify learning goals, early assessment can help by disclosing the *indicators* by which student success at the end of instruction will be measured. Students reported that gaining clarity on these indicators made a difference in how they would proceed with their studies.

Table 2-1. Strategies for Developing Clear Goals

1. Supplement goal statements, such as a syllabus provided to learners, with fuller explanations and, ideally, with a pre-test or pre-program equivalent in content and skills related to those to be assessed in the end-of-course or program (or other learning activity) assessment.

2. Engage students at the outset and again from time to time in an effort to restate goals in their own terms, and use this activity to refine their understanding and to build their commitment. Or engage students in using the intended knowledge and skills in solving problems that make the goals clear to them. Building their commitment is a key to motivation.

3. Explore at the outset whether students enrolled with different goals of their own, and explore incorporating those goals into the "contract" with each student.

4. Provide a graphic presentation of the route to goal achievement (a "concept map"). Invite student questions for clarification of the route and suggestions for making it more effective. As Step 2 (above) results in changes, revise the concept map to incorporate those changes.

5. Record and emphasize revisions of both goals and steps toward them in order to enhance motivation and understanding.

A further important question about goal-setting is: Who sets the goals? Many students expect the teacher to set learning goals. But if the teacher does so, there is a high risk that students will be less strongly motivated than if they set their own goals. Some students, more experienced as well as younger, initially insist that the instructor should dictate what is to be learned. They feel, probably rightly, that they do not know enough about the field to choose or that the instructor knows better what licensing authorities will demand. For instance, the students in Keystone Junior College's program for early childhood professionals (see their story in Chapter 4, pp. 42–43) signed on to become certified in the field. Their goal was to meet the requirements for that certification. If that goal were adopted, they would commit to whatever it involved. As these trainees gained experience and their goals changed, they were more interested in being involved in setting their own learning goals.

In some instances, such as the Ph.D. program at the University of Connecticut cited above, both instructors and students contribute to goal definition in a way that maximizes the perspectives each brings to the program. In a Ph.D. program students must develop specific research skills and gain knowledge about core theories of a field if they are to pass their General Examinations. For this reason, students look to instructors in each course for initial guidance in those matters. Each student, however, is carving out a particular research specialty. Instructors accordingly look to the students as they progress to enrich even the instructors' knowledge in those specialties.

Even in undergraduate studies some adults do want to have a voice in the more detailed choice of goals. For all students in the long run, their learning to take responsibility for their learning goals and plans is among the important objectives instructors hope students will pursue (Principle 7). In the teaching experiment mentioned above two of the 15 instructors invited students to choose the goals for a major part of their course work. In only those two cases among the 15 did a pre- and post-course measurement show gains in autonomy. The strategy of engaging students in the choice of goals is now widely used (e.g., in learning contracts, independent study courses, internships, or service-learning projects).

Aside from who wants to set goals, are there situations in which an authority *should* set the goals? In a Ph.D. program the professor teaching research methods is obligated to teach students how to become sound researchers. In the doctoral programs that today seek also to teach students how to *teach* effectively, the professor in charge of that effort should, if our theory of learning is sound, not settle for the students' becoming entertaining lecturers. In higher education each party to the teaching-learning relationship has a substantial role to play in setting goals. In professional studies that lead to licensing to practice, the instructors are obligated to make clear and to enforce the standards mandated in licensure.

Engage students in restating the goals in their own words. One way to discover whether students interpret the instructor's statement of goals with the same meaning is to have them re-state those goals in their own language. When they do so, they often articulate a different meaning than the teacher had in mind. This step can thus identify and correct misunderstandings. Removing misunderstandings early can save time and frustration for both teachers and students.

Throughout the educational innovations at Alverno College, the students were not asked to state the goals in their own words but were given tasks applying the course goals to problems in their daily lives. As they worked at these tasks, instructors could use the opportunity to build a shared understanding of the course goals. The students also became partners in choosing the route toward the desired skill development.

Explore incorporating other goals students have into a larger agenda with the teachers' goals. Find out early whether students joined the learning activity with goals of their own that are different from those the instructor has in mind. If so, there is an opportunity to "strike a deal" that will heighten the students' motivation. The deal will usually involve amending the plan of study, but may elicit even greater effort on the part of students than they would have made otherwise. Angelo and Cross (1993) report the story of a dance instructor who, not understanding an unexpectedly high level of dropouts in the second week of her course, used a questionnaire to check on the congruity between her course goals and those of the students. To her surprise she had misperceived the students' goals and, as a result, had been unaware of a mismatch with her own. Students were taking dance to improve their image and confidence and to reduce stress, whereas the teacher wanted, and had thought students did also, to improve and learn to sustain their cardiovascular fitness. Feeding this information back to students and inviting suggestions, she tried out two of the best suggestions: (1) to offer a more easily achievable skill goal for some and a more rigorous one for others, and (2) to introduce readings and discussion on self-concept and body-concept. The change made additional work for the instructor, but improved student persistence, skill levels, and satisfaction.

In content-oriented courses professors normally insist upon "covering certain material," required by licensing authorities or considered prerequisite to later courses in a discipline. To accommodate students' other interests may require some ingenuity and extra work. On the other hand, where the initial learning agreement is based on students' own wishes, as in mentor-facilitated planning of a learning contract at Empire State College, this negotiation is a built-in feature of instruction. While the students' aims are the starting-point of planning, the college's requirements for satisfying state standards for the bachelor's degree must be met by the array of learning agreements.

As learning in a field progresses, especially among students new to the field, the students' interests become clearer and often change. To sustain the higher level of motivation that sharing of goals can yield (Miller, Behrens et al. 1993), this changing of interests and focus may call for re-negotiation of the goals, at least with respect to those students who so desire.

Provide a graphic presentation of the chosen route to achieving the goal (a concept map) and invite students throughout the course to take part in clarifying and improving the plan.[2]   In a study conducted in 1997-1998 at the University of Maryland University College (UMUC), instructors were startled to discover that they were not always clear themselves as to why one stage of their course was followed by the next, nor as to how the parts reflected their own best thinking as to how to reach the course goals. Being obliged by the research design to formulate and present a "map" of the route to course goals, they naturally questioned the instruction plans and either made connections among the parts more explicit to both themselves and their students or changed the plans to make more sense (Sheckley & Walde, 1998).

A concept map is a graphic framework that shows relationships among a set of key ideas (Novak, 1995). A concept map usually takes the form of a diagram that consists of boxes or circles connected by lines or arrows. Key ideas (e.g., components of a theory in physics, rules for writing a haiku, management principles evident in a business case study) are listed inside each box or circle. To depict the relationship between the key ideas listed on the map, verbs or adjectives are written on the lines connecting the boxes. A well-constructed concept map can read as a compound sentence (Novak, 1990). In some cases a concept map represents a theory, often complex, about some aspect of the world and how it works (Kintsch, 1988).

Figure 2-1 is an example of a concept map developed by Nick Massa as part of course requirements in the Adult Learning Program at the University of Connecticut. The figure illustrates how concept maps can be used to explicate an idea, spelling out its meaning in detail and showing relationships among the elements of the meaning. Concept maps thus can help learners (a) highlight key factors related to a concept, (b) identify relationships among ideas, and (c) link information to goals (Wandersee, 1990). Concept maps help learners develop conceptual frames they can use as guides to explore problems in creative and productive ways (Novak, 1990). These maps can also help learners sort out information that is relevant versus that which is irrelevant to resolving a problem (Mellinger, 1991). In a review of research on the use of concept maps, Heinze-Fry & Novak (1990) concluded that the use of concept maps helped learners: (a) adapt information for use in a variety of situations, (b) integrate new knowledge with prior knowledge, and (c) retain knowledge about the relationships between ideas.

A concept map functions similarly to a road map (Novak, 1995). A road map differentiates between major cities, small towns, and little villages. It also shows how interstate highways, major state routes, and secondary roads link the cities, towns, and villages. Using a road map a person desiring to travel from one place to another can quickly distinguish between data in the map that are relevant to that purpose and data that are not, can see how a major or minor route leads to the

---

[2]Figure 3.1 and Figure 3.3 (next chapter) on deliberate practice are also examples of concept maps.

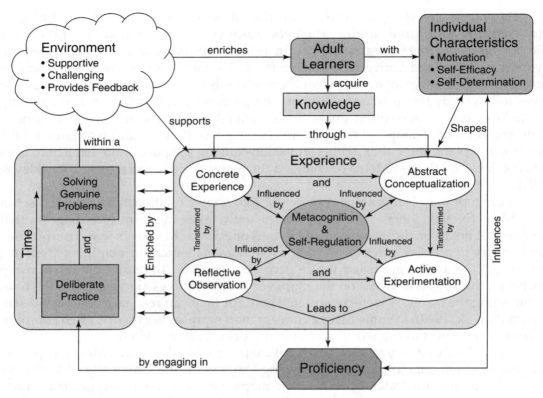

Figure 2-1. Concept map on adult learning submitted by a student in a course on Adult Learning (Massa, 2001).

intended destination, thus helping choose the best way to that place. A concept map works similarly with ideas.

Some studies indicate that concept maps enable individuals to learn by "noticing" discrepancies (McNamara, 1994). When an expectation that is implied by an idea in a concept map (or mental model) is not confirmed, the person "notices" the violation and then learns a new set of ideas to help explain the violation. Our normal idea of driving a car is that if the foot is taken off of the brake, the car slows down. Not so if one is driving a rocket ship: stopping the thruster does not slow the rocket. So noticing a discrepancy leads a person to develop a new concept that involves two different kinds of driving. In this way—developing a new concept after noticing a discrepancy between the old idea and how the world works—learners construct new knowledge (McNamara, 1994).

Research on transfer of learning indicates that information learned in classrooms usually "evaporates" within six or more weeks, possibly because it is not "deeply processed;" that is, linked to other information and uses of information already in memory (Baldwin & Ford, 1988; Ford & Weissbein, 1997). Absent such linking, the mind may hold in mind contradictory "pieces of knowledge" without noticing the discrepancies and without using all of the information available to it (Dominowski & Dallob, 1995).

The (Gick & Holyoak, 1983) story in Chapter 1 also illustrates this point about linkages and the point about human habits of putting information in segregated boxes. For the most part the participants in this study did not see the general's situation and the surgeon's as analogous, so they could not see how a concept map for reaching the goal of the surgery could be constructed with the military analogy.

The research on concept mapping indicates that it is a powerful tool for facilitating learning (Wallace & Mintzes, 1990). Further help on creating and using concept maps can be found in the Concept Map Module by D. M. Zimmaro & J. M. Cawley (1998). When instructors and learners work together to form concept maps these shared maps can symbolize not just the goal of the learning, but also the path or paths by which the learners can reach the goal.

In educational environments, the use of concept maps has evolved from paper-and-pencil to computer-based tools. A number of computer-based concept mapping tools have been reported by researchers (e.g., Fisher, Faletti, Patterson, Thornton, Lipson, & Spring, 1990; Gorodetsky, Fisher & Wyman, 1994; Flores-Mendez, 1997; Gaines & Shaw, 1995); and there exist shareware programs and even commercial products for this activity (e.g., Inspiration R, Axon R, Decision Explorer R, SemNet R). Concept mapping software offers the same sorts of advantages that word processors provide over composing written works on paper, whether revising existing work, constructing knowledge of a subject, assessing learning understanding, or the like. Computer technology, however, enables learners to go beyond paper-and-pencil capabilities and extend the capability among learners anytime anywhere. *Webster*, developed by IBM's T. J. Watson Research Center, is one such tool. Being Web-based *Webster* is accessible via a standard Web browser and allows hyperlinking from a map to the Web at large. It incorporates multimedia and dynamic nodes in addition to purely textual nodes, uses "submaps" to represent multiple levels of abstraction, supports asynchronous collaborative construction of maps by multiple students, and allows a learner to import existing maps as submaps in order to build his/her own map.

Record and emphasize revisions of both goals and paths toward them. The process of implementing Principle 1 also involves teachers and learners continually revisiting and adjusting goals and plans of study. This process helps to sustain learners' understanding and commitment. Documenting the resulting changes can help learners keep in mind what the changes are and why they were made. Angelo and Cross (1993, Part One, esp. pp. 80-82), indicate that such documentation has a positive and long-term influence on students' class work.

Concluding Note

The idea that being clear on the goals of one's learning and a way to reach them can improve results seems to be simple common sense. Knowing how to get and keep that clarity, as this chapter has illustrated, is not simple.

Being clear on the goals of a learning process is half of the job of doing the learning as long as learners maintain this clarity as the goals change or are revised. In the overall process of learning, whatever the proportion of effort this step may require, the effort is invested well because gaining clarity lowers the risk of missing the mark and enhances the chances of success.

REFERENCES

Angelo, T. A. & Cross, K. P. (1993). *Classroom assessment techniques: A handbook for college teachers.* (2nd Ed.) San Francisco: Jossey-Bass.

Baird, L. (1990). The melancholy of anatomy: The personal and professional development of graduate and professional school students. In J. C. Smart (Ed.), *Higher Education Handbook of Theory and Research, Vol. IV.* New York, NY: Agathon Press.

Baldwin, T. T. & Ford, J. K. (1988). Transfer of training: A review and directions for future research. *Personnel Psychology 1:* (1) 63-105.

Baldwin, R. G. & Thelin, J. R. (1990). Thanks for the memories: The fusion of quantitative and qualitative research on college students and the college experience. In J. C. Smart (Ed.): *Higher Education Handbook of Theory and Research, Vol. IV.* New York: Agathon Press, 337-360.

Dominowski, R. L. & Dallob, P. (1995). Insight and problem solving. The nature of insight. In R. J. Sternberg & J. E. Davidson: *The Nature of Insight.* Cambridge, MA: The MIT Press.

Fisher, K. M., Faletti, J., Patterson, H., Thornton, R., Lipson, J. & Spring, C. (1990). Computer-based concept mapping: SemNet software: a tool for describing knowledge networks. *Journal of College Science Teaching, 19:* (6) 347-352.

Flores-Mendez, R. A. (1997). Java concept maps for the learning web. In *Proceedings of ED-MEDIA '97.* Also http://www.cpsc.ucalgary.ca/~robertof/publications/edmedia97.

Ford, J. K. & D. A. Weissbein (1997). Transfer of training: An updated review and analysis. *Performance Improvement Quarterly, 10:* (2) 22-41.

Gaines, B. R. & Shaw, M. L. G. (1995). WebMap: Concept mapping on the Web. *World Wide Web Journal, 1:* (1) 171-183.

Gick, M. L. & K. J. Holyoak (1983). Schema induction and analogical transfer. *Cognitive Psychology 15:* 1-38.

Gorodetsky, M., Fisher, K. M. & Wyman, B. (1994). Generating connections and learning with SemNet, a tool for constructing knowledge networks. *Journal of Science Education and Technology, 3:* (3) 137-144.

Heinze-Fry, J. A. & Novak, J. D. (1990). Concept mapping brings long-term movement toward meaningful learning. *Science Education 74:* (4) 461-472.

Kehrhahn, M., Sheckley, B. G., & Travers, N. L. (2000). Efficiency and effectiveness in graduate education. *Association for Institutional Research Professional File 76:* 14.

Kintsch, W. (1988). The role of knowledge in discourse comprehension: A construction-integration perspective. *Psychological Review 95:* 163-182.

Magat, R. (1979). *The Ford Foundation at work: Philanthropic choices, methods, and styles.* New York & London: Plenum Press.

Massa, N. (2001). Concept map on adult learning. Unpublished manuscript Department of Educational Leadership, University of Connecticut, Storrs, CT.

McNamara, T. (1994). Knowledge representation. In R. Sternberg: *Thinking and problem solving.* New Haven, CT: Yale University Press.

Mellinger, S. F. (1991). *The development of cognitive flexibility in problem solving: Theory and application.* Department of Psychology. Tuscaloosa, University of Alabama: 1-60, 80-97, 114-167.

Miller, R. B., Behrens, J. T., et al. (1993). Goals and perceived ability: Impact on student valuing, self-regulation, and persistence. *Contemporary Educational Psychology 18:* 2-14.

Novak, J. D. (1990). Concept mapping: A useful tool for science education. *Journal of Research in Science Teaching 27:* (10) 937-949.

Novak, J. D. (1990). Concept maps and Venn diagrams. *Instructional Science 19:* 29-52.

Novak, J. D. (1995). Concept mapping to facilitate teaching and learning. *Prospects XXV:* (1) 79-86.

Sheckley, B. G., & Walde, C. (1998). Using depth of processing instructional techniques to improve learners' problem solving skills. Adelphi, MD: Institute for Research on Adults in Higher Education. University of Maryland University College.

Wallace, J. D. & Mintzes, J. J. (1990). The concept map as a research tool: Exploring conceptual change in biology. *Journal of Research in Science Teaching 27:* (10) 1033-1052.

Wandersee, J. (1990). Concept mapping and the cartography of cognition. *Journal of Research in Science Teaching 27:* (10) 923-936.

Zimmaro, D. M. & Cawley, J. M. (1998). Concept map module [Online]. Schreyer Institute for Innovation in Learning, The Pennsylvania State University. Available: http://www.inov8.psu.edu/faculty/cmap.htm.

CHAPTER 3

Use Deliberate Practice and Constructive Feedback

In a course called Introduction to Reflective Thinking one of the authors sought to help students improve their skills in deductive reasoning and in problem-solving. During initial offerings of the course the instructor designed one or two assignments that required students to use deductive reasoning and problem solving skills. The students, however, showed no improvements in these skills as a result of completing the assignments.

To address this problem the instructor decided to offer for each skill as many exercises—sometimes of rising difficulty—as needed for every student to reach mastery (100% correct if possible, but not less than 85%). Since grading and returning so much work would have been unmanageable, the instructor gave students keys for the semester's work in advance. Since the students were assured that their exercise work would not be graded, they could do the exercises and let the keys disclose where coaching was needed. As a result of engaging in assignments that provided practice with feedback on the use of deductive reasoning and problem solving skills students in the course gained 2.5 standard deviations from pre-course to post-course average on assessments.

A similar application of the strategy of frequent assessment and feedback was reported in *The Chronicle of Higher Education*, (Guernsey, 1999).

In Physics 208 at North Carolina State University students used laptop computers to complete exercises on measuring the strength of electric fields. In a practice now more commonplace, their computers were equipped with a software program that provided immediate feedback on their efforts. Students were also encouraged to consult with each other about how to solve the problems posed to them, with no two students having the exact same problems to solve. Through a process of receiving feedback as a result of their reflective dialogues with other learners "students [saw] immediately how they [were] doing in the class [in a way] that [helped] them stay motivated," instructor Risley commented (p. A22). In the process teacher time was actually saved.

These two examples illustrate Principle 2, the ideal for enhancing learning being discussed in this chapter: *Deliberate practice in the route to the goals of a learning effort will enhance and deepen the learning. Practice should be frequent and should be promptly followed by supportive feedback.*

Unpacking the Elements of Deliberate Practice

Deliberate practice involves: (a) setting explicit learning goals, (b) using assessment to diagnose achievement, (c) framing feedback to the learner using the findings of the diagnosis, (d) devising steps to improve achievement, (e) practicing hard (devoting time on task), and (f) continuing to monitor progress closely (Ericsson, Krampe, & Tesch-Romer, 1993). Diagnosing barriers, monitoring progress, and evaluating results requires frequent assessments that are valid, reliable, and efficient.

Given clear goals, deliberate practice involves the complex array of strategies and tactics outlined in Table 3-1. Such practice is not a one-time-through-and-out process, but is recursive; that is, there is frequent cycling back to repeat some or all of the steps, building each cycle upon the progress made in earlier work or, if regression has occurred, regaining what was lost.

As discussed in Chapter 2, the UCONN graduate program in Adult Learning illustrates one way these strategies and tactics can be applied. As noted in the case study, as the faculty reviewed the program they wanted to devise an effective and efficient way for students to develop proficiency as researchers. The former method—a series of research courses in which students were supposed to learn skills such as statistical analysis, qualitative methods, research design—was not working well. Most graduate students—and their advisors—knew that these one-time-and-out courses only introduced learners to certain fundamental ideas. The courses did not develop students' proficiency as researchers.

Because the main goal of the program was developing graduates who were proficient researchers the program was redesigned with a major commitment of time and resources to achieving this end. Each course was changed to provide extensive deliberate practice in conducting research. Specifically, each course was refined to address a definite research skill while also covering the content listed in the course syllabus. In each course sufficient time and resources were provided for students to collect data (using various methods such as interviews, surveys, questionnaires, etc.), to analyze data (using various methods such as statistical summaries, coding interview transcripts, etc.), and to interpret data (using inquiries such as how the results might be explained in terms of the material covered in this course). The program's commitment to deliberate practice allowed students to receive ongoing counsel, support, and feedback from faculty. This continual interaction with faculty helped students to assess their progress, celebrate their achievements, and understand the skills they still needed to develop. In each course and seminar, faculty provided learners with the resources (e.g., reading lists, access to software programs,

Table 3-1. Strategies and tactics for the Use of Deliberate Practice

Strategy	Tactic
1. Facilitate the use of deliberate practice	1.1. Allocate time-on-task sufficient to the challenge. 1.2. Time work on sub-tasks to build skills in manageable steps. 1.3. Assess gains in mastery to encourage effort, to diagnose causes of gain or loss, and to inform efforts to plan next work. 1.4. Help learners assess their own progress and become co-owners of the learning process and of the assessment findings. 1.5. Obtain help from expert assessors to assure well-grounded feedback.
2. Use feedback often, in detail, in ways that encourage continuing effort and involve students in helping themselves; i.e., be an effective mentor or coach.	2.1. Give frequent feedback and coaching in the course of practice. 2.2. In observing students' ways of learning and giving diagnostic help, use care to encourage rather than discourage their ongoing efforts to improve. 2.3. Assess, or enable the students to assess, progress on goals of each specific learning activity, and provide feedback on achievements, errors, and their causes and on next steps to further progress. 2.4. Involve students in assessing their own practice, and give needed supports and incentives for their doing so.
3. Assist students with access to needed tools and resources, and minimize the obstacles to their efficiency in learning.	3.1. Be alert to changes in tools needed, including intellectual and other resources (e.g., books, expert consultants) that can speed up or enhance learning; and provide training in the use of these resources as needed. 3.2. Re-think the use of faculty and student time to use it to best effect for learning. 3.3. Use your expertise in the knowledge area to help students find and use the best resources in the area and to teach them how to discriminate poor from good especially when buried in a mass of misinformation repetition of the same information, and irrelevant information. 3.4. Assess soundly and selectively to use time and talent most effectively. 3.5. Develop materials and activities that draw on diverse senses (visual, auditory, kinesthetic, etc.) to enhance and reinforce learning, heeding the talents and the disabilities of individual students. 3.6. Provide convenient access to instruction as to times, places, tools and equipment, and methods of learning.

etc.) they would require to complete their research. Additionally, students and faculty worked together to identify additional resources that were necessary (e.g., web links that contained information on new directions in research), best uses of time to allow for a careful analysis of research data, and creative uses of faculty expertise to assist learners in becoming most proficient as researchers. In the end this ongoing commitment to deliberate practice—and to the strategies and tactics outlined in Table 3-1—proved much more effective and efficient than did the former one-time-and-out, course-by-course method.

STRESSING DELIBERATE PRACTICE: A CLUE FROM SWIMMERS

Consider the differences among two swimmers: one who enjoys time in the pool or at the beach just for fun and one who aspires to compete in the Olympics. The two have quite different patterns of discipline and effort.

In contrast to the recreational swimmer who jumps into a pool and "just swims," the competitive swimmer has specific goals for each pool session that include measurable target achievement levels. A coach assists this swimmer in designing practice sessions in which the athlete deliberately practices specific changes in stroke, kick, or conditioning that can yield a gain in speed. Not only is the practice of the competitive swimmer more "deliberate" than that of the recreational swimmer; the competitive swimmer's practice is also more extensive. While the recreational swimmer may spend a few hours each week in the pool, the competitive swimmer may practice four or more hours per day, six or seven days a week except when "tapering" for a tournament. Unlike the recreational swimmer who just "swims," the speed of the competitive swimmer is measured day by day by stopwatch to compare results with the target; and as improvement occurs, the short-term target is changed to raise the challenge. As training progresses, the competitive swimmer and the coach watch carefully to see that there is no reversion to old, less effective habits. The long-term goal includes making best practice so ingrained that it is habitual—the individual's effective habits and capability come into play automatically. Figure 3-1 graphs the overall pattern of deliberate practice.

A recent study by Enos (2001) indicates that the process newly hired middle managers in a Fortune 500 company followed illustrated many of the patterns outlined in Figure 3-1. The process was intended to develop executive skills that helped the trainees to succeed in a new setting. In their first experiences with the company, the managers—many with graduate degrees and prior experience with other companies—were introduced to the strategic initiatives and business plans of their new company through structured activities such as briefings, presentations, and written materials. With guidance from a supervisor or an informal mentor, these new hires would work to implement plans and procedures that were in concert with the company's strategic initiatives. In many cases they added their own twist or creativity to the plans. Supervisors, colleagues, and clients all provided feedback that helped the new manager understand whether or not the plans and procedures were "on the

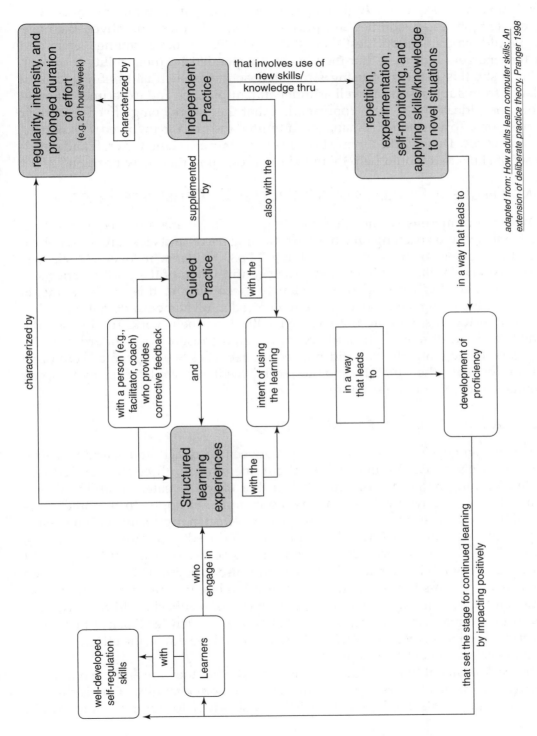

Figure 3-1. Deliberate Practice Cycle.

mark." In some cases, the new managers took on initiatives in an area outside of their current job responsibilities and prior experience. In these initiatives, the managers would experiment and test their skills and ideas in novel settings. Over and over the mangers indicated that their success depended on their ability to repeat, continuously, this process of using structured activities such as briefings, careful guidance from supervisors, as well as independent practice and experimentation to test out their ideas and to gain confirmation that they were being effective in their new positions. To a person, the managers admitted the process involved a lot of hard work and effort. They worked many hours beyond those assigned to craft and develop a set of skills that would help them to be successful in their new position.

GIVING FREQUENT FEEDBACK IN THE PROCESS OF DELIBERATE PRACTICE

There are numerous studies documenting the effectiveness of frequent assessment, feedback, and coaching on what next learning needs and tasks are most appropriate. In a review of 54 studies involving 14,689 students in over 700 classes, Lysakowski and Walberg (1982) found strong confirmation of the positive effects of feedback—especially if provided immediately. According to this review students who received ongoing feedback consistently scored a full standard deviation higher than did the students who did not receive feedback on their work. To illustrate the magnitude of this difference the authors converted the result to a standardized 100-point scale. If the students who did not receive feedback were given a score of 50 points on the scale, the students who did receive feedback would score a whopping 33 points higher (83) on the scale.

DISCOURAGING VS. ENCOURAGING FEEDBACK

In a meta-analysis of the relationship between feedback and learning gains, Kluger and DeNisi (1996) found that in about one of every three studies feedback impeded learning because it discouraged further effort, threatened students' self-esteem, or was perceived by students as too complex to apply. In the other two-thirds of the studies, feedback had a large, positive effect in producing learning gains because it focused attention on students' progress, induced goal setting (Principle 1), pinpointed do-able efforts to improve, and offered advice on ways students could improve their work. Kluger and DeNisi found also that immediate and written error-correction is less likely [but not necessarily] to be interpreted by learners as a commentary about their personal capabilities than oral feedback. Additionally, as in the North Carolina State experience reported above, written feedback is positively motivating. Feedback, then, should be tailored to avoid the downside effects just listed and to elicit its potential benefits.

Feedback is meant to help students understand what they are and are not doing correctly, but various factors can interfere with this understanding. One is the student's reasoning habits. Suppose that a teacher wishes to help students avoid invalid

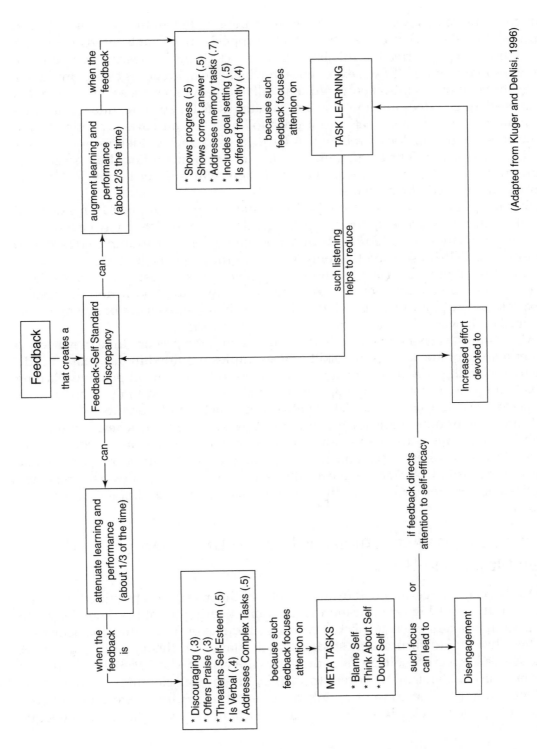

Figure 3-2. Effective feedback.

Feedback

that creates a

Feedback-Self Standard Discrepancy

can → augment learning and performance (about 2/3 the time)

when the feedback

* Shows progress (.5)
* Shows correct answer (.5)
* Addresses memory tasks (.7)
* Includes goal setting (.5)
* Is offered frequently (.4)

because such feedback focuses attention on

TASK LEARNING

such listening helps to reduce

can → attenuate learning and performance (about 1/3 of the time)

when the feedback is

* Discouraging (.3)
* Offers Praise (.3)
* Threatens Self-Esteem (.5)
* Is Verbal (.4)
* Addresses Complex Tasks (.5)

because such feedback focuses attention on

META TASKS

* Blame Self
* Think About Self
* Doubt Self

such focus can lead to

Disengagement

or

if feedback directs attention to self-efficacy

Increased effort devoted to

(Adapted from Kluger and DeNisi, 1996)

Effectiveness and Efficiency in Higher Education for Adults   27 deductive inferences. One invalid pattern to be avoided is that of thinking that affirming the "then" clause of an "if . . . then" proposition warrants inferring that the "if" clause is true. Correcting this habit can be a challenge. A teacher will look for examples in the student's own experience in which the inference is clearly mistaken. For example, if one is mistakenly told that "all antihistamines are safe for treatment of sinus allergies," does it follow that a medication safe for such treatment is an antihistamine? Some students feel sure it does follow. Or if all cows are animals and Growler is an animal, does it follow that Growler is a cow? As the reader can easily conclude, Growler might be a monkey, a dog, or a mountain lion. But "seeing the point on this case" does not mean that the insight will transfer to, say, a false "if" clause and a related "then" clause.

Sternberg and Wagner (1986) report that subjects perform poorly on examples outside of their practical experience—precisely the area in which it may be most useful to have firmly embedded habits of sound deduction. For example, Wason and Johnson-Laird (1972) showed that only 15% of a group of college students correctly deduced the solution to an abstract numbers problem. In contrast, when the students were asked to use the same principles of deduction in a situation within their realm of experience (i.e., they were asked to deduce which individuals in a bar were under-age drinkers), over 75% of the students reasoned correctly.

Many times teachers do not provide students with the practice time they need to master a body of knowledge or a skill. The examples provided in this chapter indicate that allowing adequate time for such practice often results in positive learning gains that more than offset any adjustments that were required in the plan of work for the course or the division of labor between instructor and students.

With contemporary tools for providing feedback, however, teachers can provide feedback more efficiently than before. For example, in Web enhanced courses students can complete exercises and receive feedback via built-in scoring. In online courses that provide a practice-and-feedback feature, faculty can oversee repeated practice and provide prompt feedback more easily than in traditional face-to-face forums.

PRACTICE DIVERSE APPLICATIONS OF IDEAS TO UNDERSTAND THEIR MEANING-IN-USE

As chapter 7 (page 101) will discuss, much of the instruction provided in American institutions of higher education focuses on covering a field of knowledge. In doing so instructors often neglect to provide students opportunities for deliberate practice that would insure that students understand the theory fully (Harvey & Knight, 1996). Alverno College takes the view (site visit of May, 1998), that a student does not fully understand a concept (principle, finding, or scientific law) unless the student can apply that concept appropriately in at least three quite different contexts. This policy is clearly an important application of Principle 2 on deliberate practice. One cannot determine whether an adequate understanding of a concept has been achieved by simply using tests of recall of narrative knowledge, be they tests by way of essays or standardized tests. For example, in their study of pilots (Stokes, Kemper & Kite, 1997) demonstrate that while both high and low experienced pilots may achieve high passing scores on paper and pencil tests, the high experience pilots who have practiced most deliberately will outperform low experienced pilots in actual in-flight simulations. (Here Principle 2's emphasis on sound assessment comes into play.)

Many of us have had students who were brilliant in reciting abstract theory, but who did not have a sensible grasp of ways to apply that theory in different situations. This matter of learning how to apply "the material" appropriately is a major part of the students' becoming an effective learner. It is never too early to start the practice that can develop this kind of understanding.

INVOLVING STUDENTS IN ASSESSMENT OF THEIR OWN PRACTICE AND GIVING NEEDED SUPPORTS FOR THEIR DOING SO

Deliberate practice may involve a combination of self-regulated and teacher- or coach-directed efforts (Ericsson & Lehmann, 1996). Both skill development and memorization require repetition if the gain in skill or knowledge is to be embedded and built upon.

With a teacher in a subject-matter oriented course, practice may occur by use of the newly acquired knowledge in a discussion, in an essay assignment, or in a test of knowledge. A common weakness of courses of this type is the failure on the part of instructors to provide sufficiently frequent occasions for practice in any form. As students move from introductory-level studies to courses that require higher order thinking skills and more advanced knowledge, similarly to the swimmer who moves to a higher level of competition, the complexity and the difficulty of the practice necessary to master these new skills will increase. In the writing of professional-level papers the practice may take the form of rewrites of a single paper. In a senior seminar for philosophy majors with a goal of defining a policy to govern ethical practice, the instructor required four presentations from each team of students, with other students giving feedback at each step before the last and with the instructor providing feedback at all four steps. A "library" of selected sets of these drafts (called "standards files") was used to guide future students and to demonstrate to accrediting teams that high standards were being achieved.

RECOGNIZING AND ADDRESSING OBSTACLES TO EFFECTIVE USE OF FEEDBACK

Another major obstacle to ideal use of critique is students' defensiveness or students' response that criticism of specific learning activities is an attack on the worth or competence of that student (Kluger & DeNisi, 1996). No reasonable teacher will offer criticism with such intent, but in the attempt to make meaning of feedback a student can perceive a teacher's well-intentioned assessment as a negative statement about that student's capabilities. A teacher may prevent much of the dysfunctional response to feedback by early attention to the ground rules for constructive criticism and for its productive use in that the feedback: (1) it underscores progress, (2) it provides a correct answer, (3) it makes connections with concepts already learned, (4) it includes specific goals, and (5) it is provided frequently (Kluger & DeNisi, 1996).

RE-THINKING THE USE OF FACULTY AND STUDENT TIME

Since the examples of deliberate practice and of feedback just discussed have been about cases in which the instructors were staying within normal time commitments to their courses (most rigorously enforced in the formal experiment), the instructors made time for students and themselves by lessening work on other aspects of instruction (lecturing or group discussion) to provide time for deliberate practice.

> *The senior author underwent an especially trying, but instructive, experience of re-ordering his use of time on one occasion. In one semester of an extended study one section of a philosophy of religion course was more than four times as large as usual with 95 instead of the normal 22 students per section. This was a course in which each student wrote five essays (ten to fifteen pages in length normally) that had to be critiqued in writing and graded by the instructor. It was clear at the outset that with 95 students something "had to give." Taking a tip from a professor at Oberlin College, the instructor asked students to work in teams of four to critique one another's essays and to select, seek consensus, and explain why one of the four best fulfilled each of the criteria for good writing stated in the syllabus. In addition, to reduce instructor time in class as required, some instructor time was taken to train student discussion leaders and recorders in seven break-out groups that met concurrently once or twice per week. In all sections of the four-year study, this section alone showed higher achievement on the final assessment of essay work than its control section did.*

The example illustrates the great value of having students work collaboratively in groups (Principle 5 to be discussed later) to practice deliberately the skills they are learning. These students gained experience in critiquing writing and developed their own mental models of how it can be done. Some of them commented to the psychometrician monitoring the study that they did not agree entirely with the instructor's criteria for good writing but that they could adapt to his expectations or write to satisfy their own.

In these times of demand for containing the costs of higher education, this study and that with physics instruction cited earlier in this chapter yield a highly important finding: They both illustrate ways to elicit more and more lasting learning at lesser cost. This efficiency can be achieved by substituting more productive use of teacher and student time rather than by adding to their workload. In other words, instructors must work more intelligently, often more creatively, but not longer. To be specific, replacing 20% of a teacher's time in preparing and delivering lectures with activities that enable students to assess their progress and to take greater responsibilities in helping one another learn is an example of more efficient teaching practice.

ASSESS SOUNDLY TO USE TIME AND TALENT MOST EFFECTIVELY

While assessment and feedback are important as means to the end of improving the pace and outcomes of instruction, the assessment must be soundly done if it is to be a reliable guide to improvement. In an effort to strengthen the assessment, a team of three faculty members in Accounting at UMUC who taught sections of the same course spelled out their measureable learning objectives with two further steps: (1) for each objective they stated indicators that would indicate the level of achievement on the objective and agreed that performance on these indicators would be measured by all course instructors; (2) for each indicator they defined three different levels of complexity (in Bloom's taxonomy) to clarify the goal of higher order thinking, and (3) for each indicator they devised at least three different ways (tools, procedures) by which performance could be measured, with each instructor free to choose among these ways. As Kluger & DeNisi (1996) show, feedback from assessment can be misleading if poorly done. For instance, if the feedback fails to clarify the learning goal or fails to identify promising ways to come closer to its attainment, it may lead to wasted effort on the part of the learners. In addition, if the assessment deals only with lower order skills (memorization as against analysis, for example), it can fail to advance the students' long-term needs.

College instructors are often not experts in measurement. Rarely do they have the time and resources that are spent by psychometric organizations to develop valid and reliable instruments: tests, interview protocols, or rules for refereeing performance assessments. To the suggestion that ordinary grading might be used more frequently for the needed level of assessment and feedback, it must be observed that faculty often intend their grades to combine measurements of progress in learning with recognition of the levels and effectiveness of participation, with promptness in turning in assignments, and with other matters that do not relate well with what is being learned. As a result, grades are normally poor indicators of what has been learned. If they are reported as reliably indicating student achievement and thus institutional effectiveness, an evaluator may be misled about the institution's effectiveness. Ideally the institution would have clearly stated overall learning goals, as does Alverno College, to which each course contributes.

How can the need for valid measurement (measuring what is intended) and reliable measurement (measuring it accurately and consistently over time) be assured when instructors have the other time pressures they do? Here again there is often confusion on the part of instructors as to what they should be assessing. Only by freeing up time they would otherwise spend on less productive work can the clarity and competence for good assessment be assured. Similarly, the authenticity of student work can be effectively monitored within teachers' limited time if steps taken early in a course familiarize the teacher sufficiently with students that the distinctive marks of each one's work can be discerned in later work. In addition, aids to detecting plagiarism are now available through the Internet.

Among the ways to save instructor time-on-assessment is that of adopting and adapting the work of others. A coalition formed and led by Dr. Lawrence Kelley of Northeastern Louisiana University is engaged in just such sharing. This sharing can focus on assessing institution-wide learning outcomes, such as achievements on the general education goals of the institution, or on the learning outcomes of specific teachers' courses. Using this exchange for the former purpose, a faculty member newly assigned to develop for his institution an assessment program for introductory level general education objectives asks others on-line about two specific nationally normed instruments. A number of others in the listserv have experience with the instruments—some finding one or the other highly useful and suited to the institution's aims, but others unsatisfied. The exchange provides help in articulating the features to be investigated before a choice is made.

PROVIDING CONVENIENT ACCESS TO INSTRUCTION AND THE MEANS TO ITS BEST USES

American higher education has made great strides in the past two decades in providing convenient access to instruction for students wherever located and of whatever backgrounds (Flint & Associates, 1999). The idea that academia should be in a retreat setting removed from easy reach of the bustling center cities has yielded to the greater need for interplay with the places where learning is applied and for holding down the costs of accessing instruction (CAEL, 2000). The ways to provide such access are many, but the necessity of making that provision is now a given in the management of institutions of postsecondary education. In using emerging telecommunications technologies, the requirements of access to tools and knowledge about how best to use them are essential to most effective and efficient learning. A typical online course will be delivered with the support of a "platform," software that provides a framework for activating different kinds of learning activity: receiving reading or writing or project assignments and returning them for critique, conferencing (discussion groups on line), study groups (often 4 to 7 students carrying out projects or writing tasks), chat rooms (for synchronous discussion that may be socializing and bonding rather than doing assigned work), and teacher-moderated discussions of main themes of the course. Here, as with face to face classes, it is important to assure substantial practice and constructive feedback.

REFERENCES

CAEL (2000). *Serving adult learners in higher education: Principles of effectiveness.* Chicago: Council for Adult and Experiential Learning.

Enos, M. (2001). *How managers develop proficiency: The role of informal learning.* Unpublished Ph.D. dissertation, Department of Educational Leadership, University of Connecticut, Storrs, CT.

Ericsson, K. A., & Charness, N. (1997). Cognitive and developmental factors in expert performance. In P. J. Feltovich, K. M. Ford, & R. R. Hoffman (Eds.): *Expertise in context: Human and machine.* Cambridge, MA: MIT Press.

Ericcson, K. A., Krampe, R. T., & Tesch-Romer, C. (1993). The role of deliberate practice in the acquisition of expert performance. *Psychological Review, 100:* (3) 363-406.

Ericsson, K. A., & Lehmann, A. C. (1996). Expert and exceptional performance: Evidence of maximal adaptation to task constraints. *Annual Review of Psychology, 47,* 273-305.

Flint, T. A., & Associates. (1999). *Best practices in adult learning: A CAEL/ APQC benchmarking study.* New York: Forbes Custom Publishing.

Guernsey, L. (1999). Textbooks and Tests That Talk Back. *The Chronicle of Higher Education, XLV: (23),* A 21-22.

Harvey, L., & Knight, P. T. (1996). *Transforming higher education.* Buckingham, UK: The Society for Research into Higher Education & The Open University Press.

Kluger, A. N., & DeNisi, A. (1996). The effects of feedback interventions on performance: A historical review, a meta-analysis, and a preliminary feedback intervention theory. *Psychological Bulletin, 119:* (2) 254-284.

Lysakowski, R. S., & Walberg, H. J. (1982). Instructional effects of cues, participation, and corrective feedback: A quantitative synthesis. *American Educational Research Journal, 19:* (4) 559-578.

Sheckley, B. G., & Walde, C. (1998). Using depth of processing instructional techniques to improve learners' problem solving skills. Adelphi, MD: Institute for Research on Adults in Higher Education, University of Maryland University College.

Sternberg, R. J. & Wagner, R. K. (1986). *Practical intelligence: Nature and origins of competence in the everyday world.* Cambridge University Press.

Stokes, A. F., Kemper, K., & Kite, K. (1997). Aeronautical decision making, cue recognition, and expertise under time pressure. In C. E. Zsambok & G. Klein (Eds.): *Naturalistic decision making.* Mahwah: Lawrence Erlbaum Associates.

University of Maryland (1997). *Teaching at a distance: The online experience.* Technical report, Institute for Research on Assessment in Higher Education (IRAHE), University of Maryland University College, College Park Maryland.

Wason, P. C., & Johnson-Laird, P. N. (1972). *Psychology of reasoning.* Cambridge, MA: Harvard University Press.

CHAPTER 4

Balance Challenge and Support for Learning

The Mathematics Department of the University of Wisconsin at Madison was trying in the early 1990s to have a larger proportion of enrollees complete a sequence of calculus courses (Math 111, 221, and 223) and develop increased confidence in their mathematical abilities. In 1993-1994, with primary funding by the National Science Foundation and a supplemental grant from IRAHE, the faculty carried out a controlled experiment using the emerging scholars approach developed by Professor Uri Treisman at the University of California-Berkeley (Treisman, 1990). The Berkeley program was an honors program for underrepresented students that provided challenges in the form of difficult worksheets and supports by way of student-driven work groups. The model had a history of successes at a wide range of institutions that served very different student populations.

The Wisconsin Emerging Scholars (WES) Program sought to use the model successfully in a predominantly Caucasian, research-oriented setting with regular teaching staff. The institution enrolled non-honors as well as abler students. Half of the WES students were women, 40% from underrepresented ethnic minorities, and primarily entering first-year students.

The Calculus 111 students met in large lecture sections (about 300 students) three times a week for 50 minutes. Control sections of 20 each met an additional two times a week for 50 minutes each time with a graduate teaching assistant (TA). The TAs reviewed the lecture and, at student request, worked problems on a blackboard.

The experimental sections met three times a week for two hours each. Students earned two additional credits for successful completion of the requirements. The experimental sections also met in the workshop room informally whenever they wished, had the option of residing on the same dorm floor with one another, and were invited to a few social events. They did problems that were both more difficult and more carefully designed than the homework assignments, worked on the problems together in groups of three or four, and could get hints from the TAs when frustrated—but were never helped directly to solve the problems. They had to answer the questions themselves.

The experimental group completed the first two semesters of calculus with grade point averages more than a half grade higher than students in the control sections. This result held even when measures of pre-college mathematical and general academic ability were statistically controlled. The advantage of WES students generalized across sub-groups of various types, including women and minorities. The experimental students also showed high levels of confidence in their mathematical ability and greater comfort in performing calculus problems, learned to value multiple and creative ways of problem solving, and developed interest and ability in acquiring a deeper conceptual understanding of calculus. The WES approach appeared, in the eyes of the research team, "robust, independently of personalities or setting."

Researchers Susan B. Millar, Blaine B. Alexander, Heather A. Lewis, and Joel R. Levin attributed the success to the combination of challenging worksheets, extended work times (time on task), functional groups (collaborative learning), flexible workspace for workshops, supportive but not intrusive instructors, and peer-like senior peers (the TAs)(Millar, Alexander, Lewis & Levin, 1999).

Background

Since World War II, student bodies in American colleges and universities have become increasingly heterogeneous in age, ethnicity, educational objectives, and patterns of participation (Clark, 1970; Cubeta, Travers & Sheckley, 1999; NCES, 1997). The numbers of working adult students have burgeoned from tiny proportions to more than 25% of the population in numerous public universities. When student bodies were of uniform age, had common family educational backgrounds, and shared similar goals, a standardized pattern of admissions and of requirements for progressing toward a degree was quite workable. That pattern of general introductory courses followed by a prescribed curriculum is now less and less appropriate to good use of the time of students and professors. It violates a key learning principle:

Balancing the challenge of high expectations with supports tailored to the individual learner's needs in meeting the challenge can yield increased learning and persistence (Principle 3).

This principle can be implemented by four strategies and related tactics that we will discuss in this chapter (see Table 4-1).

Table 4-1. Strategies for Balancing Challenge and Support

1. Provide an early opportunity for assessment of learners' prior knowledge and skills, and recognize their starting condition with appropriate standing, credit, placement, or remedial work.

2. Develop a profile of the learners' characteristics that signal high or low risk and tailor the level of challenge relative to risk for each learner.

3. Raise the level of performance expected from that encountered earlier by the current learners, but not beyond a manageable level.

4. Tailor the supports to the weaknesses or difficulties posed by the challenge presented and the learners' profiles.

DISCOVERING THE BEST STARTING POINT FOR LEARNING

To present an appropriate level of challenge for learners, instructors must find out "where the learner is" at the outset. Efficient instruction begins with the level of skills, depth of knowledge, and breadth of experiences an individual brings to a learning situation (Willingham, 1977). Actually, instruction cannot begin at any other point. As this declaration suggests, if the instruction is to be most effective, the instructor or an agent acting on behalf of the instructor should, as early as feasible when students begin their college studies or training and certificate programs, do a valid and reliable assessment of students' learning up to the point of entry (Willingham & Associates, 1976). This assessment should include both school-based and out-of-school learning. If time and money are not to be wasted, the institution will use this assessment of what students already know and can do to place students appropriately and, within that placement, to design instruction to match the needs.

Initial placement can be done in different ways. In some cases institutions provide remedial instruction for underprepared students. In other cases, some students can be given advanced standing either by allowing them to skip over introductory courses or by awarding academic credit that translates their prior learning into the credit structure of the institution. If the nature, depth, and breadth of a student's learning revealed in this initial assessment can be equated with a course name and number, instructors can then get a reasonable picture of a student's starting point (Willingham, 1977).

The process of determining appropriate initial placement will vary for different institutions. Testing to achieve appropriate placement in respect to reading, writing, and numeracy is commonly done by an office serving an entire school. In disciplinary courses it is more common for a course instructor to use a pre-course task, a test, or an initial assignment to get the picture of a student's initial readiness.

An estimated 48% of colleges and universities in the United States provide an individualized comprehensive "prior learning assessment service" to evaluate claims by students that they have creditable knowledge and capabilities in the disciplines (Zucker, Johnson, & Flint, 1998). At UMUC during 1995-2000 among students opting to use this service, the average semester hour credit award was between 19 and 20 credits. As working adults who normally take one or at most two courses per term, these students saved 2 to 3 years toward degree completion and avoided wasting time going over material already mastered. A study funded by the Institute for Research on Adults in Higher Education (IRAHE) at UMUC compared completers of the UMUC prior learning assessment course (EXCEL 301) over a four year period with all students who did not take the course. The EXCEL completers required fewer years to graduate, had superior grades in their courses, and, in spite of having received 19-20 credits on average for non-school learning, took more additional courses with UMUC (Hoffman, 1999).

A first step in appropriate placement helps students understand both what they *do* know and what they will be required to learn in order to earn a degree (Willinghanm, 1977). Once the student and the faculty have the same picture in mind as to what needs to be learned, progress is made easier and success more likely. Lacking that understanding, misunderstanding and difficulty may continue. For example, if doctoral students think that they need only conduct a research study and write it up for their dissertations—and do not realize that they are meant to make a new contribution to theory in the field—they are likely to encounter difficulties in completing their program of study.

GETTING A PICTURE OF A STUDENT'S PROMISE

Given a student's starting point in terms of a program of studies, a second essential of effective and efficient instruction is to know what characteristics of the student present a risk to success in the program and what characteristics offer promise of success. Those who work with the student to plan a program of study will need to evaluate the factors making for risk of failure and promise of persistence on students' educational goals.

Research has disclosed significant differences between college students most at risk of dropping out or failing on one hand and those of highest promise to persist and succeed on the other hand (Kennedy and Sheckley, 2000). Learners who persist and succeed know when and how to seek help. They also believe in their ability to succeed academically, have a sense of being able to control events, and feel accepted as legitimate members of the learning community. Successful learners typically have relatively few stressors in their lives that detract from their studies (Cubeta, Travers et al., 2001).

First among the factors just listed was habits of help-seeking. It is a troubling fact that an offer of help can be received by a poor learner as a triply adverse put-down (Karabenick and Knapp, 1991). First, this learner is encumbered by a vast history of marginal academic success. Second, this history reinforces low expectations about future success. Imagine, third, the threat of asking for help and still finding out that you cannot succeed. Often individuals most in need of help (e.g., students with grades below C-) report that the prospect of not succeeding after receiving help is a strong deterrent to seeking help in the first place. This strategy of doing without the needed help is, of course, self-defeating. Such students are reluctant to ask fellow-students for help and even more reluctant about acknowledging their need to teachers (Karabenick and Knapp, 1988). A first way to reduce the risk of failure is for students to learn that help-seeking is encouraged and is a mark of good students.

Highly successful students, who have a past history of success and a strong belief in their ability to do well, on the other hand, are likely to view it as a feather in their caps if they can shorten time on task and learn better by getting someone else's help within the ground rules against cheating. From things they learn in this way, they can extract a lesson about learning methods and resources and can apply the lesson to different future tasks.

In a research study at UMUC on ethnically diverse students (Caucasian, Hispanic, African-American, Asian-American) this difference between more and less effective learners was found to hold across ethnic lines (Cubeta, Travers et al., 2001). Students with low grade-point averages (GPAs) were differentiated from those with high GPAs by the level of their help-seeking, with the more successful students seeking help more frequently. The adverse effect of less help-seeking students had a larger effect size than did the positive effect for high performers (Cubeta, Travers et al., 2001). Whether this difference holds more broadly than with the UMUC population, we do not know.

Once the picture of students' risk factors and that of their starting situations in the field of study are available, teachers and student support staff can tailor expectations and supports to the needs and resources of each student. For example, at Prince George's County Community College (PGCCC) in the 1990s a task group was searching for better ways to help at-risk students persist toward promising careers. The task group combined the use of in-house PGCC records with results of the 1991-1996 UMUC Study of Risk and Promise to identify ten distinct groups of students highly likely to drop out early. The PGCC Office of Institutional Research selected for an experiment two groups with maximum remedial needs (i.e., below-college level in reading, writing, and mathematics) but with other characteristics favorable to persistence (level of confidence in self as learner, well-developed help-seeking habits, relatively high ability levels, and an internal locus of control). An intervention called the R-Cubed Academy was designed that provided a "homeroom" for the students' classes, an adjacent space for socializing, and two instructors devoted entirely to these two groups. The instructors used these settings to provide an array of supports similar to those described in the WES program described at the beginning of this chapter. After two semesters 84% of the entering students in the experiment were still in the program, as contrasted with similarly characterized previous groups that had lost more than 50% of their members after only the first semester (Keeton, Clagett, & Engleberg, 1998). The experiment illustrated the powerful effect of holding out hope for better-than-earlier performance with support tailored to the characteristics of the particular students (Clagett & Engleberg, 1999).

APPROPRIATE PLACEMENT: RAISE EXPECTATIONS TO AN ACHIEVABLE LEVEL FOR EACH STUDENT

Insightful teachers have long heeded the practice of starting instruction from the foundation already achieved by their students. In 1878 a professor at Johns Hopkins University shocked colleagues by admitting the young Abraham Flexner, not just as a first year student, but with senior standing, on the basis of learning that he had demonstrated in an oral examination. The good sense of the professor's judgment was confirmed by later events. Flexner, in the early 20th century, became the principal author of standards for American medical education.

A common practice in astute placement is that of discovering students' current reading levels and reading interests and then assigning next reading tasks that will interest and challenge the students at just the right level (Renzulli, 1988). This practice fits with that noted earlier of using "placement examinations" in reading, writing, and mathematical skills to determine who needs "remedial" work or who can benefit from advanced placement. (Phipps, 1998) reports that while remedial education in the late 1990s used less than 1% of the budgets of public institutions, these programs benefited institutions in terms of increased retention rates. The programs also helped students to develop skills that provided a foundation for future success. Nevertheless, controversy arose in the late 1990s as to whether this service should be offered by universities or only by secondary schools and community colleges. With increasing enrollments of adults in postsecondary education, Phipps' report suggests that remedial education programs may become more prominent. According to Phipps (1998) most of the students served were over 22 years of age (more than a quarter over 30); such work has saved even larger costs in time and money in avoiding poor placements.

When students are studying online, they need to have telecommunications equipment suited to that of the host college or university and to be proficient in its use. The adequacy of this fit will have a significant impact on the time required to perform adequately and possibly on the level of their success in the online courses.

The effects of assessment-based individualized placement upon learners who have used it have been dramatic (Zucker, Johnson, & Flint, 1998). The utility of courses and workshops that teach students how to present and document their claims is still being researched through efforts of centers such as the Institute for Research and Assessment in Higher Education (IRAHE) at the University of Maryland University College. Typical average credit awards for an institution of higher education are between 17 and 20 semester hours (Zucker, Johnson, & Flint, 1998). Users of this type of service report with high frequency that the credit awards were less important to them than the discovery that they had the capability for college-level work and the clarification for them of what remained to do to earn more advanced credentials. Many more awardees then successfully undertook the more advanced studies than would otherwise have dared to try.

To summarize, if an institution uses the strategy of early assessment of students' starting qualifications and appropriate placement, the ensuing benefits include teachers' and learners' understanding of where the learners begin, what the students' goals are, and what the institution will require to reach them. As with a competitive swimmer's first time trials, they enable teacher and learner to have a new clarity and specificity about the tasks ahead.

BALANCING THE CHALLENGE WITH MATCHING SUPPORTS

Given a picture of a student's risk and promise, teachers do not have an easy task of setting a challenge that enhances learning. An optimal challenge needs to embody a reasonably higher expectation than the learner has faced before, but not so high as to be unattainable within the period available and with the resources that are accessible (Rigby, Deci et al., 1992). Vygotsky (1979) describes such challenges as falling within "the zone of proximal development"—an area where a student cannot perform a task alone but can do so with the guidance and assistance of a teacher. Think, for example, of a novice pilot preparing for his/her first solo flight. A skillful flight instructor will guide this novice through the zone of proximal development by providing challenges (e.g., stalling the engine while in flight) and supports (e.g., showing the novice how to restart the engine while avoiding a deadly spin) until the novice is ready to fly solo. Whether students are learning to fly or to understand advanced calculus, for each challenge they encounter, instructors need to provide supports to help address the challenge. This combination of strategies (outlined in Table 4-1, p. 37) is widely espoused, but less commonly implemented.

High expectations rigorously implemented can dramatically increase the achievements of students (Roueche & Roueche, 1993). Given the diverse factors that enter into effective and efficient learning—program challenges, student's characteristics, institutionally-provided supports, and teacher talents—creating a strategy that achieves an optimal *balance of challenges and supports* is a complex task. According to a host of researchers (Chickering, 1976; Knefelkamp and Sleptiza, 1976; Knefelkamp, Widick et al., 1978; Weathersby and Tarule, 1980; Rigby, Deci et al., 1992) the challenge must evoke a best effort and highest aspiration from the learner. The support must be sufficient to bring this goal within the reach of the learner's capability, commitment, energy, and persistence.

LINKING ADMISSIONS POLICY WITH APPROPRIATE PLACEMENT

One way this challenge-support balance is struck is to match admissions policy on "selectivity" with the level of challenge the faculty present to the students. Three different choices in striking this balance are common. Each is appropriate to specific circumstances and each requires that implementers tailor supports appropriately to the challenge being presented:

- admit all who need a program, and build supports to enable them all to meet the challenges provided by the program; or
- set a high challenge for the program and select for admission only those students who have the skills and abilities to meet this challenge; or
- admit students with a diversity of readiness and capability, then individualize the level of challenge and the supports students will need to achieve success.

Figure 4-1 presents these options graphically. Some colleges are highly selective but provide low levels of supports for students (e.g., some Ivy League colleges). In contrast other colleges (e.g., Community Colleges) follow an open admissions policy and provide strong supports for students to achieve success. Both approaches can be effective because they provide an appropriate balance of challenges and supports. The least desirable situation in terms of enhancing student learning is for institutions to adopt a high level of challenge in its academic programs, admit students who may not have to preparation to meet the challenge, and offer no supports to assist these students. This combination offers a ready-made formula for failure. It would not effectively boost student learning nor would it represent an efficient use of institutional resources.

When an institution adopts an open admissions policy for a program of study, the institution must provide supports and services to accommodate "at-risk" students who may apply. A good example of this approach is the 1990-1992 Keystone Junior College (PA) program to prepare early childhood development paraprofessionals. In this program most of the students had been on welfare. At the start of the program students took three competency-based core courses. Teachers provided a 40-unit modular format. An added course in field experience enabled the students to satisfy requirements for a Child Development Associate certificate. The supports provided (e.g., remedial instruction, individualized instruction, group assignments,

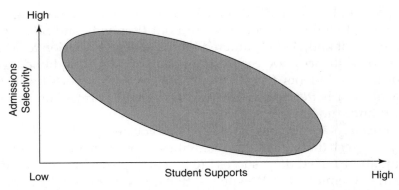

High

Admissions
Selectivity

Low   Student Supports   High

Figure 4-1. Relationship between selectivity of admissions and academic supports for students.

etc.) reduced attrition rate for the experimental group to 25% from the 42% drop-out rate that is usual for the program. Graduates were also successful in their jobs upon graduation (Shaffmaster & Langan, 1999).

In this type of program the level of difficulty of the learning tasks can be adjusted in light of the supports students need and the resources the institution can feasibly provide. Keystone Junior College was able to build significant challenges into their program (e.g., skills that must be developed to qualify for licensing) because of the inherently high level of motivation provided by the opportunity for paid employment for the welfare recipients in the program.

Given that the match between the demands of a program upon students and their abilities, interests, and readiness can be a major factor in the learning and professional development of the students, institutions should take care to admit only students who have reasonable prospects of being able to meet the demands. This caution is especially warranted if the institution has an open admissions policy but program demands cannot be mitigated to accommodate ill-prepared students or if high demands are chosen for other reasons.

Most colleges balance level of selectivity with the challenges and supports included in their programs of study. They do not have large enough applicant pools to be highly selective and do not need, on the other hand, to admit only students at high risk. Such institutions tend to admit as many applicants as they think can benefit and then to tailor supports, either individually or by groupings of students, to meet their diverse needs. For such institutions, the recommendations of Roueche and Roueche (1993) are especially appropriate. These researchers advocate "proactive pre-enrollment activities that personalize the college by addressing primary concerns early on." Most colleges, however, defer what we call "matchmaking" processes until *after* admission, in part because such activities entail out-of-pocket costs before a commitment is made by the student to pay tuition. Since colleges spend an average of between $1500 and $2000 per student in recruiting and approximately 40%-60% of students eventually drop out (Kennedy and Sheckley 2000), the timing and degree of knowledge gathered for the college's decision to admit students have serious consequences. We regard the policy of "deciding blind" as ill-chosen. Colleges who assess students' fit with the challenges and supports the institution provides will achieve a better return (i.e., greater retention rates) on the investments made in recruiting students.

A more effective admissions strategy is advocated by Roueche and Roueche (1993). They suggest that orientation activities should include activities that will build a foundation for student success (e.g., early provision of remedial help on weaknesses in academic skills). We suggest that this kind of activity begin during the pre-enrollment stage of the admission processes. One of the partner institutions in UMUC's Diverse Students Program, Cambridge College, reported that use of this pre-enrollment strategy enabled them to achieve an 85%-90% graduation rate for its undergraduate degree-completion students. To implement this strategy the college encouraged students who applied and were "tentatively" accepted to enroll in a special workshop. In this forum students worked with their advisors to craft a detailed plan in which study, financing, and support services were matched with course demands, with the students' learning readiness, and with the students' own work-family-study situations. The contributions of the sessions to persistence, to degree completion, and to warm working relationships were substantial.

Initial planning for students' ability to pay a first semester's or first year's tuition is a virtually universal practice, but doing so for the entirety of the students' expected years with the college, as happened with the special workshop described above, is often neglected. While some students will say, "One step is enough for me," long-term success is more likely if the distant outlook is also appraised *from the start*. This policy is especially appropriate when the costs of higher education are increasing more rapidly than household incomes.

IDENTIFYING APPROPRIATE SUPPORTS

As already reported in the Wisconsin Emerging Scholars Program, students persisted and succeeded in unprecedented numbers when innovative support in "lab sections" was instituted (Millar, Alexander, Lewis & Levin, 1999). A different, but highly effective, pattern of challenge and support is reported in Janke & Myers (1999):

The UMUC Nuclear Science Program

An unusual way of providing critical support is illustrated by the UMUC Nuclear Science Program for active employees of nuclear power plants. The program came about in response to the meltdown at Three Mile Island. A 1979 ruling of the Nuclear Regulatory Commission (NRC) mandated that all senior reactor operators must hold a bachelors degree by 1991. Later the requirement was reduced to a recommendation. The feasibility of operators earning the degree, how-ever, was questionable given the hours and shifts each employee worked.

The UMUC addressed this educational need by creating a consortium of UMUC, UMCP (University of Maryland College Park's Nuclear Engineering Department), industry consultants, and four nuclear utility companies (Balti-more Gas & Electric, Louisiana Power & Light, South Carolina Electric & Gas, and Wisconsin Public Service). A survey indicated that an ideal program would include a strong engineering base augmented by education in management. The plants' operating schedules (around the clock seven days a week) and shift rotation presented a special challenge. Additionally, since the plant had to undergo planned, and sometimes unplanned, refueling and repair outages, workers some-times worked up to 16 hours a day. The academic backgrounds of operators were also diverse.

To cope with these challenges, OSP delivered instruction onsite at the plants rather than requiring employees to come to campus. Instructors made four onsite visits per three-hour course, repeating class sessions multiple times during a two to three day visit. The on-site visits were supplemented with computer-assisted instruction at a distance that provided for asynchronous communication among students, between students and instructors, and between students and the site coordinator. OSP also provided academic and technical support. Seven academic disciplines were involved in the project. Classroom work was supplemented fur-ther by the use of journals, directed writing, instructors meeting face-to-face with students having difficulty, and collaborative learning tasks.

The program began in 1984 on one site with 40 students. By 1994 it was enrolling 600 students in 9 states at 15 different sites. Students and faculty reported enhanced student learning as compared with alternatives and a higher proportion of students succeeding. Costs, all paid by employers, were $20,000 per student/program as compared with $100,000 or more for alternative provisions. (Jahnke & Myers, 1999)

When students are admitted into an academic program such as the Nuclear Sci-ence Program just described, supports must be put into effect immediately. These supports can be built into both teaching practices (courses, workshops, and other learning experiences) and "student support services." Creative approaches (e.g., mentoring programs) may combine teaching, advising, and key student services into one activity. The research literature (Delworth & Hanson, 1980; Knefelkamp, Widick & Parker, 1978; Rouche & Rouche, 1993) suggests such specifics as: (a) establishing a mandatory policy for basic skills assessment followed with placements in appropri-ate courses, (b) providing critical safety nets for students (e.g., faculty mentors, peer mentors, cohort activities, and collaborative learning), (c) requiring teachers to include problem-solving and literacy activities in all courses, and (d) providing sup-plemental instruction and tutoring as an integral part of normal instruction.

Whether the goals and objectives adopted in a program provide an optimal challenge depends in part on the level of such supports that the learners receive. The WES Program described at the beginning of this chapter provides one model for balancing challenges and supports. Other ways can also be devised. For instance, the Supplemental Instruction Program of University of Missouri at Kansas City (Wilcox, 1999) is based on the premise that there are no at-risk students, rather there are high-risk courses. For such courses, the University provides a supplemental support system that significantly raises the odds of student success. The support system uses student "coaches" who provide group tutoring and supervised practice directed toward enabling the students to learn how to attack and solve the assigned problems. In both the Kansas City and the Wisconsin cases, students traditionally viewed as at-risk achieved higher than usual success rates.

Tailoring Instruction as Well as Supports

How did instruction in more successful programs differ from that in the less successful ones? The more successful programs were distinctive in the ways they combined the use of learning principles described in this book. In many cases the more successful programs used a combination of Principle 3 on challenge and support, Principle 5 on the benefits of collaborative reflection, and Principle 8 on the effects of a climate of inquiry. In the successful ventures (e.g., the WES example), students engaged in learning actively. Students in these courses thought through problems and solved them independently. Learners received hints or avoided false leads by seeking help from one another, a teacher, or an assistant. Students in these courses were responsible for their own learning. In the less successful efforts students were most often listening and watching as someone else (teacher or assistant) did problems. Students in such courses usually do not take control of their own learning. Instead they tend to look to the teacher for direction on what to learn, how it is to be learned, and for resolution of all problems that may interfere with learning (Travers and Sheckley 2000).

Adapting to Different Program Requirements

How can the principle of appropriate supports be applied in a sound manner in a wide range of higher education programs? Some programs use early diagnostic assessments coupled with remedial or developmental services to "bring up to speed" all entrants who otherwise would not succeed. Some programs use this diagnostic work to counsel unprepared students to use an educational alternative for which they are ready and to help them develop better strategies for learning. Some provide special supports for entrants who almost, but not fully, meet the minimum standards for the program. Most astute educators try to avoid putting unprepared or under-motivated students into situations in which they are, as the expression goes, "programmed for failure."

One illustration of an excellent application of this strategy is the developmental math program, the developmental reading program, and the developmental writing program at Alverno College (Mente, 1999; Bowne & Engelmann, 1999; Witkowski & Magness, 1999). Each of these programs offers supports that match the needs of entering undergraduate students. These programs also engage the students in collaborative efforts to learn how better to learn.

College educators often overlook the need to provide "developmental" preparation when students move from introductory college studies to a more advanced level. Alverno College recognized that such support is often required to assure that students are ready to benefit at each stage of a program. By adopting a college-wide curricular change that emphasized the development of higher-order cognitive skills, the faculty addressed the needs of students who had done well in introductory courses, but were not effectively making the transition to intermediate level ones. The faculty combined early diagnosis of difficulties students were encountering at the more advanced level with interventions specific to each discipline. The interventions included the use of journals, directed writing, conceptual linking, and collaborative learning. The faculty also provided extensive feedback on individual performance.

Research on student success suggests that after pre-course assessment of skill and readiness levels has taken place, the best instructional strategy may be to tailor instructional demands and supports to assist some of the more challenged students while requiring other students to participate in developmental courses (Long & Amey, 1993; Schwitzer, Grogan, Kaddoura, & Ochoa, 1993). An alternative approach is to include the use of instructional aides as well as an integrated use of instruction, counseling, and tutorial services.

Sometimes students need help with starting academic skills (reading, writing, math, and study habits) as well as help in raising confidence in themselves as learners (Cubeta, Travers et al., 2001), help in linking the learning under way with their own strong interests (Travers and Sheckley, 2000), and help with their habits of persistence (Kennedy and Sheckley, 2000). Most educators know of instances in which a bright, determined student has succeeded against seemingly insurmountable odds, even in a context of poor teaching and unsupportive family or community. Such cases are an exception. More often, students who are at-risk of failing need substantial help in bolstering their belief in themselves as learners, with development of basic skills, and with their strategies for self-regulation (Zimmerman and Kitsantas, 1997).

While training in study skills is sometimes a useful step for at-risk students, more fundamental is the help of a teacher, adviser, or counselor in raising the confidence level of individuals in their ability to learn (Delworth & Hanson, 1980; Feldmann, Martinez-Pons et al., 1995). For example, the supports provided in the WES project had a salutary effect on students' self-efficacy and self-regulation. In addition students in the program reported increased aspirations for further work in Calculus. Classroom assessment activities such as those reported in Angelo and Cross (1993) also offer clues for individualizing instruction while also sustaining achievement on course goals (e.g., having students submit on index cards at the end of class issues that are confusing them). Since education is inherently a process of development, this balance of challenge and support must be continually reconsidered and adjusted (Chickering 1976; Knefelkamp, Widick et al., 1978).

Problems of match and mismatch between program demands and student capabilities may increase when an institution as a whole offers "open admissions" while particular programs are selective (Cross, 1971). Selectivity, moreover, may not always focus on such criteria as scholastic aptitude. The Keystone Junior College program for displaced homemakers is an example of trying to develop a group of such students who can progress together through a degree and certification program more expeditiously than in the usual kind of entering collegiate cohort (Shaffmaster & Langan, 1999).

ENGAGING PRACTITIONER FACULTY

A great many universities and community colleges engage as adjunct faculty people whose day-by-day work roles are those of manager, researcher, editor, lawyer, physician, surgeon, nurse, school superintendent, or any of a great number of other professional roles. Increasingly today universities and hospitals collaborate in providing instructors for degree programs in the health care fields, whether or not the hospital is university-owned-and-operated. An employer may realize a financial advantage by contributing staff time as well as the use of equipment and facilities in a way that saves costs and other inconvenience to the employees who are studying.

The case study "Six Strategies for Efficiency" (Porosky, 1999) illustrates how the use of adjunct faculty can be integrated into an overall strategy for efficiency. This strategy is especially appealing to mature students who are already employed and want to advance in their careers quickly. They appreciate having instructors who are practitioners of state-of-the-art performance in their specialties. This preference is found especially in degree and certificate programs for paraprofessionals and professionals in disciplines such as law, health occupations, human services, management, and teaching. At UMUC practitioners who are actively applying the research findings they discuss in class provide virtually all graduate instruction. Graduate Schools sometimes overlook the value of faculty practitioners who are also expert teachers preferring instead to hire energetic practitioners of research who sometimes are less energetic or competent practitioners of teaching.

How do the UMUC practitioner faculty make learning more efficient? The answer appears to derive at least in part from the distinctive kind of expertise they bring to their instructional efforts and to its effects upon student interest and motivation. Conveying abstract knowledge usually does not bring with it an understanding of how to put that knowledge to work in concrete situations (Ford and Weissbein, 1997; Rigby, Deci et al., 1992). Sometimes the full-time academic has less applied knowledge and normally less interest in it than has the practitioner.

Engage Employers in Planning and Evaluating Learning Outcomes. One of the most common complaints of businesses about college and university graduates is that they are not ready to perform adequately in the workplace in matters for which they are supposed to have been prepared. A good way for colleges and universities to insure against complaints of this nature is to engage the employers in program planning from the outset. Such planning could also elicit assistance from the employer in designing the evaluation of the graduates' qualifications just prior to degree completion.

The frequently found deficiency that students have the words for, but not the meaning of ideas in application, can be avoided if the workplace is used as a testing-ground for demonstration of mastery-in-use. Gates and McNault (1993), for example, found that individuals who learned on-site at their place of work significantly outperformed individuals who learned the same skills in a course based at the university.

Internships in management and in many other fields of study can be used in such evaluation of program outcomes. For students currently working for a collaborating employer, the practice also makes for saving of time and other costs. Concurrent work and study programs of Antioch University in its McGregor School and its Los Angeles, Seattle, and New England Colleges achieve these results by a variety of arrangements: internships in clinical psychology, practica in the management of nonprofit enterprises, assistantships in teaching, and the like.

Beginning in 1995, a number of industry-wide associations of employers have collaborated in issuing, in cooperation with the U.S. Departments of Labor and Education, sets of proposed voluntary national occupational skills standards. Some of these will be suited to mastery in secondary education, where educators are organized in DECA. Others will require education at the community college level or higher. Collaboration between educational institutions and employers in evaluation of employees' skill levels can save money and assure the enforcement of high standards more readily than can a pattern of staying at arm's length among these potential collaborators.

A Concluding Note

Trying to start instruction at any point different from a point based on a learner's prior knowledge and experiences will be a recipe for wasted effort, unnecessary costs, and frustration. To avoid these woes, instructors and their academies need systematic ways of assessing the students' starting points. Selective assessment of basic academic skills is highly desirable, but insufficient.

Once knowledge of students' readiness for college work is in hand, focus is needed on providing significant challenges for further learning. Where the students lack confidence, learning skills, and other related strengths, colleges should also provide supports that give them reasonable prospects for success. As illustrated in the stories cited, there are many ways to meet these conditions.

REFERENCES

Angelo, T. A. & Cross, K. P. (1993). *Classroom assessment techniques: A handbook for college teachers.* (2nd Ed). San Francisco: Jossey-Bass.

Bowne, P. & Engelmann, D. (1999). Improving effectiveness and efficiency in teaching and learning for intermediate students (Alverno College). In M. T. Keeton (Ed.): *Efficiency in adult higher education: Case studies.* Adelphi, MD: Institute for Research on Adults in Higher Education.

Chickering, A. (1976). Developmental change as a major outcome. In M.T. Keeton (Ed.): *Experiential learning: Rationale, characteristics, and assessment.* San Francisco: Jossey-Bass.

Clagett, C. A. & Engleberg, I. N. (1999). The R-Cubed Academy at Prince George's Community College (MD). In M. T. Keeton (Ed.): *Efficiency in adult higher education: Case studies.* Adelphi, MD: Institute for Research on Adults in Higher Education.

Cross, K. P. (1971). *Beyond the open door: New students to higher education.* San Francisco, Jossey-Bass.

Cubeta, J., Travers, N., & Sheckley, B. G. (2001). Predicting academic success of adults from diverse populations. *Journal of College Student Retention: Research, Theory & Practice, 2:* (4) 297-313.

Delworth, U. & Hanson, G. (1980). *Student services: A handbook for the profession.* San Francisco: Jossey-Bass.

Feldmann, S. C., Martinez-Pons, M., & Shaham, D. (1995). The relationship of self-efficacy, self-regulation, and collaborative verbal behavior with grades: Preliminary findings. *Psychological Reports, 77:* 971-978.

Flint, T. A., & Associates (1999). *Best practices in adult learning: A CAEL/ APQC benchmarking study.* New York: Forbes Custom Publishing.

Ford, J. K. and Weissbein, D. A. (1997). Transfer of training: An updated review and analysis. *Performance Improvement Quarterly 10:* (2) 22-41.

Hoffmann, T. (1999); Legrow, M., & Sheckley, B. G. (1999). Making prior learning assessment pay its way: Three case studies. In M. T. Keeton (Ed.): *Efficiency in adult higher education: Case studies.* Adelphi, MD: Institute for Research on Adults in Higher Education.

Jahnke, T. & Myers, A. (1999). Cost effectiveness in a UMUC nuclear science program. In M. T. Keeton (Ed.): *Efficiency in adult higher education: Case studies.* Adelphi, MD: Institute for Research on Adults in Higher Education.

Karabenick, S. & Knapp, J. (1988). Help-seeking and the need for academic assistance. *Journal of Educational Psychology 80:* 406-408.

Karabenick, S. & Knapp, J. (1991). Relationship of academic help-seeking to the use of learning strategies and other instrumental achievement behavior in college students. *Journal of Educational Psychology 83:* (2) 221-230.

Keeton, M. T., Clagett, C., & Engleberg, I. (1998). Improving minority student success: Crossing boundaries and making connections. Adelphi, MD: Institute for Research on Adults in Higher Education.

Kehrhahn, M., Sheckley, B. G. & Travers, N. L. (2000). Efficiency and effectiveness in graduate education. *Association for Institutional Research Professional File, 76:* (14).

Kennedy, P. & Sheckley, B. G. (2000). Dynamic nature of student attachment to college: Influences on persistence. Association for Institutional Research National Forum, Cincinnati, OH.

Knefelkamp, L. & Sleptiza, R. (1976). A cognitive development model of career development: An adaptation of the Perry scheme. *The Counseling Psychologist 6:* (3) 53-58.

Knefelkamp, L., Widick, C., & Parker, C. (1978). *Applying new developmental findings.* San Francisco: Jossey-Bass.

Legrow, M. & Sheckley, B. G. (2000). Educational benefits of completing a portfolio of prior learning. Paper presented at the International Conference of the Council for Adult and Experiential Learning. Chicago: IL.

Loevinger, J. (1976). *Ego development: Conceptions and theories.* San Francisco: Jossey-Bass.

Long, P. & Amey, M. (1993). A study of underprepared students at one community college: Assessing the impact of student and institutional input, environmental, and output variables on student success. Paper presented at the Annual Meeting of the Association for the Study of Higher Education, Pittsburgh, PA, November 4-10. [ERIC ED365177].

Mente, S. (1999). Course innovations in developmental math (Alverno College). In M. T. Keeton (Ed.): *Efficiency in adult higher education: Case studies.* Adelphi, MD: Institute for Research on Adults in Higher Education.

Millar, S. G., Alexander, B. B., Lewis, H. A., & Levin, J. R. (1999). The Learning through evaluation, assessment, and dissemination/engagement (LEAD) project. In Keeton, M. T. (Ed.): *Efficiency in adult higher education: Case studies.* Adelphi, MD: Institute for Reseach on Adults in Higher Education.

National Center for Educational Statistics (1997). *The pocket condition of education.* Washington, DC: US Department of Education.

Phipps, R. (Ed.) (1998). *College remediation: What it costs, what it is, what's at stake* [On-line], 38 pages. Available: *http://www.ihep.com/Remediation.pdf* [March 29, 1999].

Porosky, J. (1999). *Six Strategies for Efficiency in Learning.* In M. T. Keeton, (Ed.): *Efficiency in Higher Education: Case Studies.* Adelphi, MD: Institute for Research on Adults in Higher Education.

Renzulli, J. S. (1988). The multiple menu model for developing differentiated curriculum for the gifted and talented. *Gifted Child Quarterly, 36:* (4) 298-309.

Rigby, C. S., Deci, E. L., Patrick, B. C., & Ryan, R. M. (1992). Beyond the intrinsic-extrinsic dichotomy: Self-determination in motivation and learning. *Motivation and Emotion, 16:* (3) 165-185.

Roueche, J. E. & Roueche, S. D. (1993). *Between a rock and a hard place: The at-risk student in the open-door college.* Washington, D.C.: The American Association of Community Colleges.

Shaffmaster, L. & Langan, F. G. (1999). The early childhood educational professional preparation project: A case study in adult learning (Keystone Junior College). In M. T. Keeton (Ed.): *Efficiency in adult higher education: Case studies.* Adelphi, MD: Institute for Research on Adults in Higher Education

Travers, N. & Sheckley, B. G. (2000). Changes in students' self-regulation as related to different instructional approaches. Association for Institutional Research National Forum, Cincinnati.

Treisman, P. U. (1990). Mathematics achievement among African-American undergraduates at the University of California, Berkeley: An evaluation of the mathematics workshop program. *Journal of Negro Education, 39:* (3).

Vygotsky, L. S. (1979). Consciousness as a problem of psychology of behavior. *Soviet Psychology, 17,* 5-35. (Original work published in 1925).

Weathersby, R. & Tarule, J. (1980). Adult development: Implications for higher education. Paper presented at the National Conference of the American Association for Higher Education: Washington, D.C.

Wilcox, F. K. (1999) Supplemental instruction: Review of research concerning the effectiveness of SI from the University of Missouri-Kansas City and other institutions from across the United States. In M. T. Keeton, (Ed.): *Efficiency in adult higher education: Case studies.* Adelphi, MD: Institute for Research on Adults in Higher Education.

Willingham, W. W. & Associates (1976). *The CAEL Validation Report.* Princeton, NJ: Cooperative Assessment of Experiential Learning.

Willingham, W.W. (1977). *Principles of good practice in assessing experiential learning.* Princeton, NJ: Cooperative Assessment of Experiential Learning.

Witkowski, S. & Magness, D. (1999). Integrated language practice: Efficiency and effectiveness in learning (Alverno College). In M. T. Keeton (Ed.): *Efficiency in adult higher education: Case studies.* Adelphi, MD: Institute for Research on Adults in Higher Education.

Zimmerman, B. J. & Kitsantas, A. (1997). Developmental phases in self-regulation: Shifting from process goals to outcome goals. *Journal of Educational Psychology 89:* (1) 29-36

Zucker, B. J., Johnson, C. C., & Flint, T. A. (1998). *Prior learning assessment: A 1996 survey of American institutional practices.* Chicago: CAEL.

CHAPTER 5

Broaden the Experience Base and Reflect Actively Upon It

T he history of science is one of learning. That learning came about by broadening observations, by arranging conditions to elicit more telling observations, and by reflecting upon ways of using those observations to expand knowledge and theory. A notable example of inquiry that involved reflection on experience is the familiar story of Copernicus' "discovery" that the sun rather than the earth is the center of what we now call the solar system. The story is familiar, but how the reasoning involved was seen then and now is widely forgotten.

> Ptolemy believed that the earth was the center, not only of the system of nearby planets, but of the entire universe. On the basis of church teachings, he also thought that the circle was the perfect motion. For this reason, Ptolemy and others thought that the orbits of the planets deviated from circularity only because of other forces acting upon them. When they could not observe such forces, Ptolemy and his fellow astronomers hypothesized that unobserved "epicycles" were at work to cause these deviations. As observations of those planets, the sun, and other stars accumulated, however, astronomers had increasing difficulty explaining the motions of the planets by the Ptolemaic hypothesis, especially given Ptolemy's belief that all motions of heavenly bodies embodied the perfect motion of circles. Improvements in the instruments of observation only compounded the complexity of explanation needed to account for actual planetary paths. The added data did not flatly contradict Ptolemy's theory; they merely made it more difficult to reconcile with the facts.

> To arrive at a better explanation of the available data, scientists were not content with simply accumulating more observations. Copernicus searched for a different frame of reference to organize the observations, to discern their import, or to assign them new meaning. Upon reflection, he conceived the idea that the sun might be the center of the planetary system. This insight came from imagining alternatives to the present explanations and then selecting one that explained the data more economically (with fewer unconfirmed assumptions). Copernicus'

hypothesis had another advantage: it made it possible to predict the presence of a then undiscovered planet (later named Pluto, its status as a planet being contested now that still other similar small bodies have been found) and to estimate its location and mass.

Advances in science have occurred as a result of work by researchers such as Copernicus who reflected on their observations, confirmed their ideas with calculations that made use of mathematical tools, and used their imaginations to devise further ways to test their theories. As with these scientists of the past, learners today also benefit from the interplay between growing experience and critical reflection that yields further knowledge.

Can this reliance upon accumulating experience and reflecting upon it critically be effective in advancing learning in messier enterprises than science, say in higher education? Arthur Morgan thought so. In 1919 Antioch College, which had gone bankrupt under the management of the YMCA, was searching desperately for a new president when Morgan heard of its plight. He was encouraged by General Motors' executive Charles F. Kettering, Sr., to take the job.

Morgan's idea was to have students alternate periods of book learning with periods of hands-on experience in employment. Morgan, who did not himself have a college education, thought that this format would prepare students to solve genuine and significant problems. For students to hone problem-solving skills, Morgan believed that they had to experience them first hand and then spend time discussing these problems with scholars. He was aware that the University of Cincinnati had been using such a curriculum since 1912 in its engineering and management departments. Morgan proposed to apply the idea to the education of generalists or to what has come to be called general education or liberal education. The result, as briefly sketched in the case example that follows, has been a highly productive institution of higher learning.

> *Beginning in 1921 students at Antioch College have alternated full-time work with full-time study. Since that time the faculty has experimented with different lengths of study and work periods. The initial five-week periods made it difficult for students to have jobs at a large distance and to achieve the depth in either work responsibility or study that seemed best. Combinations that filled the year with minimum vacation time created high levels of stress and required that faculty be unavailable for at least one study period per year. A calendar of two 8-week and two 12-week periods was less efficient than calendars of four 11-12 week periods. In some arrangements students of the two-divisions (called A Division and B Division) were sometimes on campus together, with the consequence that in other periods campus facilities were not fully utilized.*
>
> *The primary purpose of the alternating work and study, known as cooperative education, was effectiveness in education (combining scholarly reflection with*

practical experience). A major secondary purpose was financial efficiency. This arrangement, for example, permitted a ratio of 19 or more student tuitions per faculty member while the classroom ratio was only 14 to 1.

External investigators have done a number of studies of Antioch's educational effectiveness. In the 1950s a committee of the faculty of Wesleyan University carried out studies on the production of Ph.D.s among graduates of liberal arts colleges. Antioch was among the highest producers of doctorates in the natural sciences, the social sciences, and the humanities (Knapp & Goodrich, 1952; Knapp & Greenbaum, 1953). Alexander Astin (1962, p. 134) later used these and other results in identifying Antioch as one of the "overproductive" colleges. He found that traditional measures (e.g., SAT scores, socio-economic class, ethnicity, gender) did not explain this growth. A study by Phillip E. Jacobs (1956) also reported substantial effects on the Antioch students' values.

The financial efficiencies derived from serving two student bodies with a single faculty, plant, and equipment. The presence of two student bodies indistinguishable from one another in key variables made the institution highly attractive for the conduct of educational experiments.

The Center for the Study of Higher Education of the University of California-Berkeley (UCB) carried out a longitudinal study of eight postsecondary institutions—including Antioch. The project explored how and why students selected the institutions, what the students were like when they started, and what happened to them while at the institution. This study reported (Clark, 1970) greater change in values at Antioch than at the other colleges studied (for example, impulsivity scores on the Omnibus Personality Inventory fell among Antioch students from 91st percentile at entry to the low 60s at graduation—a "cooling off" effect). At the same time the performance of seniors from Antioch on the Graduate Record Examinations was better than their performance had been on SATs at entry.

Since the late 1970s Antioch has been designated a university by the Ohio Board of Regents. The home college based in Yellow Springs, Ohio, continues to require alternating work and study of all undergraduates. Four other colleges of the University serve older adults, the great majority of whom are working full time. These students use concurrent work and study, live relatively near the college's base (Keene, NH; Seattle; Los Angeles; Yellow Springs), and attend classes mostly on weekends or on lengthy evening sessions two or three times weekly.

Experience and Reflection

Broadening one's experience base and reflecting critically upon it are essential for learning to occur optimally (Principles 4 and 5). The stories from the history of science and from the use of alternative and concurrent work and study at Antioch University illustrate how these principles can be applied.

Principle 4. A rich body of experience is essential for optimum learning. Those who engage in direct experience of an object of study will normally learn more accurately and penetratingly about it than those who do not experience it directly.

Principle 5. Experience yields explicit (narrative) knowledge only if actively reflected upon. Such reflection often occurs best in interaction with peers, instructors, or other active questioners. Reflecting upon one's ways of reflection can yield a double benefit by enhancing a learner's power to learn.

Abundant research evidence shows that experience coupled with reflection enhances learning. So crucial to the development of expertise is the extent and diversity of experience accumulated that Ericsson, Krampe, and Tesch-Rimer (1993) say that at least ten years of sustained, full-time experience are required to attain an international level of expertise in many callings. In a comparison of experiential versus lecture-based methods of instruction in an accounting class Specht and Sandlin (1991) reported that students who engaged in experiential methods (e.g., problem solving exercises, reflection on action, formulating generalizations from experiences, applying principles to new situations) scored over a full standard deviation higher than their cohorts in the lecture-based sections on measures that assessed understanding and retention of concepts over time. Van Eynde and Spencer (1988) also reported that students in a management course who were taught using experiential methods, in contrast to learners in lecture sections, scored a full standard deviation higher on assessments of long term memory and use of concepts taught in the course. In a study that documents the power of reflection on experience Legrow and Sheckley (2000) found that learners with years of business experience who engaged in a structured process of reflecting on the learning they acquired from their prior experiences (i.e., they completed a portfolio that documented their prior learning) developed more complex solutions to a real-life business problem than did a comparable set of students who participated in a lecture-based classroom course.

As suggested by these research findings, adult learners bring a great advantage to learning by virtue of their having accumulated more knowledge from experiences in more diverse contexts than have younger persons (Sheckley & Keeton, 1997a). In addition, adults' extensive encounters with problems requiring complex reflection typically result in greater complexity of thought and better developed problem solving skills than less experienced learners have (King & Kitchener, 1994; Kitchener & King, 1981). Even with the wide differences in backgrounds of younger versus older students, colleges typically focus almost entirely on developing their students' grasp of generalizations and theory. To apply principles 4 and 5 effectively, colleges may have to alter this one-size-fits-all approach. With younger students collegiate programs could focus more on increasing the range and variety of those students' experience. Older adults, who tend to be "experience-rich and theory-poor," may need a heavier emphasis upon reflection and critique of their prior experiences. Because of these differences in students' backgrounds, the mix of reflection and experience in their respective programs of study should be tailored to the different backgrounds among students at entry (Keeton, 1977).

Explicit knowledge, expressed in language, is a product of experience and reflection (Schacter, 1996). Lacking experience, there is no knowledge of the world (Damasio, 1999). Some experiences, however, can be more instructive and memorable than others (LeDoux, 1996). Touching a hot stove with the bare hand, for example, seems to produce lasting knowledge with a minimum of reflection. Extensive experience can also produce tacit knowledge—knowledge of which the knower may be unaware and cannot fully put into words, but can nevertheless apply effectively, as in experts' knowledge of "the tricks of the trade"(Reber, 1993). In this chapter we explore these relationships as to how Principles 4 and 5 can be applied to the improvement of instruction.

Applying Principle 4: Broadening the Experience Base

It is really our minds, not just our eyes, that experiences open (Edelman & Tononi, 2000). The following tactics may be used, singularly or in combination, to achieve that benefit.

- Increase the amount of the learner's experience with the object of study (i.e., the idea, concept, skill, or item that is the focus of inquiry).
- Diversify the types of experience the learner is encountering that are relevant to the inquiry. Wherever feasible, engage learners in hands-on experiences (percepts) to complement their vicarious exposure to the experiences of others (precepts others have derived from their own experience). Simulations can also broaden learners' awareness of the world.
- Focus the learners' growing experience base upon those opportunities likely to expose them to new social contexts, types of problems, or types of creative applications of knowledge.
- Avoid the major obstacles to building a superior experience base (i.e., not attending to key aspects of an experience). Make sure the learner encountering novel situations is aware of, is seeing, hearing, and sensing the most relevant aspects of the experience.

A VARIETY OF WAYS TO BROADEN EXPERIENCE

Experience teaches in small matters as well as large. Working adults, especially those with more than five years of experience with the range of adult responsibilities, bring an advantage in the databases for their studies but also in experience with effective and ineffective efforts to reflect on them. A number of today's adults have had experience in the Peace Corps or in domestic versions of service learning or internships that significantly broadened their awareness of the subcultures of this country and of one or more cultures abroad. One of the great benefits of alternating work and study in college is the help that first hand experience of work situations gives students in clarifying career choices earlier than would happen if they went all the way through the bachelor's before "testing the waters." For example, such was the experience of a student who first wanted to prepare to be a medical doctor, but had stronger interests in the plastic and graphic arts than in applied biology or chemistry and had shown far more talent in the arts than in the hard sciences. She learned from an early experience as an aide in a Chicago hospital that she could not tolerate what surgical aides had to endure.

Another of the benefits of experience-rich instruction is its effect in promoting social and intellectual development in the learners. Conrad and Hedin (1991), comparing lecture-discussion methods with experientially-enriched instruction, say:

> Researchers consistently report a heightened sense of personal and social responsibility, more positive attitudes toward adults, more active exploration of careers, enhanced self-esteem, growth in moral and ego-development, more complex patterns of thought, and greater mastery of skills and content that are directly related to the experiences of the participants [in the experientially-enriched instruction] (p. 147).

In research on gaming as a route to learning, Coleman (1976) reported that learning that takes place through acting (or observing others act) and then experiencing the consequences (which Coleman termed "experiential learning") has effects different from those of classroom learning in which knowledge is imparted by an instructor (which Coleman termed "information assimilation"). Experiential learning and information assimilation each has its advantages and its disadvantages, he went on. For instance, information assimilation depends heavily upon understanding of the language. According to Coleman (1976), the heavy dependence on language mastery required for assimilative learning may result in difficulties if a student does not completely understand the words being used, uses words to construct defective chains of associations, or processes information erroneously due to defects in the way words and their associations were stored in memory. This disadvantage applies particularly for learners who are "culturally disadvantaged" (as with those learning in English for whom it is a second language) "for such disadvantage lies largely in linguistic and verbal skills" (p. 55). Astute orchestration of the use of both information processing and experiential learning is therefore an important strategy for optimizing learning.

In their studies of "reflective judgment," which at higher levels entails more demanding standards of evidence and reasoning to reach a warranted judgment about what is factual or what is a better course of action, King and Kitchener (1994) found that adults 35 years of age and older had, even without benefit of college or graduate study, reached levels of judgment comparable to those of graduate students who were younger. These superior levels of reflective judgment appear to us to be a product of greater experience and the effects of being responsible for the results of earlier misjudgments.

Why, we may ask, do employers often require earlier job experience and offer higher pay to applicants with more extensive experience and responsibility in their background? It is, of course, because the employers believe that the more experienced workers: (a) will know more and be more skillful in doing the work, and (b) will have disclosed by their record of performance how proficient they are. The process of accumulating experience and for learning from it (via reflection) will have furthered the learning of the older applicant. This expectation holds whether the job is playing professional football, managing personnel functions in a business, or being a successful marketer of products. In some jobs the product of past experience is a grasp of the theory of the work, but in many the most important value of prior experience is that kind of knowledge that the worker may be unable to articulate, but can demonstrate in performance—tacit knowledge (Broadbent, FitzGerald & Broadbent, 1986). Examples of tacit knowledge abound among expert performers: how to break free on the gridiron to catch a pass and tack on yards after the reception; how to give criticism to an employee in a way that does not evoke resentment but results in observable improvement; or how to get things done in a given organization or situation. All of us have accumulated tacit knowledge at less expert levels: about how to drive a car, how to manage our money, and how to get along within our family.

When it comes to skills development, there is simply no substitute for repeated practice (Principle 2)—that is, for a large body of experience in doing the task (Ericsson, Krampe et al., 1993). For example, cooperative education programs can save instructional time on campus by having students learn chemistry laboratory skills on a job requiring weeks of practice of the basic skills in the use of instruments.

At the level of more sophisticated study, breakthroughs in research, whether in physics and other hard sciences or in the social sciences, require a study design that produces experience under novel conditions controlling variables in hitherto untried ways. The resulting experiential data can then be "processed" (i.e., reflected upon critically) in ways that yield original knowledge (Kolb, 1984).

Experience can, of course, teach the wrong things. Why do so many students, of whatever age, enter college lacking confidence in themselves as learners? Generally they have had discouraging experiences as learners and have mistakenly inferred that they are incapable of doing better. Obversely, they lack experiences of succeeding as learners. A research program of UMUC's IRAHE documents that low levels of confidence in self as learner are predictive of high risk of failure in college (Cubeta, Travers, & Sheckley, 2001). Since some experiences are productive of useful learning, there is a need at every age for care in the design and conduct of instruction to see that it at least does no harm. Winter, McClelland and Stewart (1981) reported that some colleges' seniors were less skillful in critical thinking than were the freshmen, a regrettable experience indeed. Surely instruction should enhance the learners' ability to continue learning successfully.

COMMON DIFFICULTIES IN BUILDING A SUPERIOR EXPERIENCE BASE

There are genuine and substantial obstacles to the building of a superior experience base via college or university education. Seven such difficulties stand out in the authors' experience.

Many instructors in college are preoccupied with "covering the material." This concern leads to a search for ways to cover as much as possible as quickly as possible. Naturally spending more time memorizing the narrative knowledge of a field speeds up covering the material; but it does not normally embed such learning in long-term memory nor improve the learner's ability to apply the knowledge appropriately (Sheckley & Keeton, 1997b). One cause of the poor retention is that the knowledge does not come out of the learner's own experience; the knowledge derives from others' experiences—not nearly as memorable as one's own (Damasio, 1999). In such learning the student does not experience what is being talked about and may as a result build a vocabulary without really knowing what it means—the student "has the words, but not the melody."

A further obstacle to building a superior experience base is the costs in time and money of enlarging one's experience base. We might still be living in trees if we had to learn *everything* from personal experience. A teacher can report in a few minutes all that was learned by others in weeks or years of encounters with "the real world." A student can even get this knowledge quickly by reading what the first-hand experiencers inferred from their experiences. The inferences may be different from what the student would have inferred, but using them does save time and money—and does accelerate the students' learning.

A further complication in building an ample experience base is that few of the most important possible interactions with the world can be realistically pursued in classrooms. There are exceptions, of course: e.g., listening to a native speaker in a foreign language or practicing speaking oneself in the presence of such an informant, or practicing public speaking before an audience of classmates. In science laboratories in colleges the so-called experiments are often not genuine investigations, but are "cookbook experiments," in which the student attempts, not to achieve new knowledge or to challenge accepted theory, but to "get the same results" as professionals have attained in their expertly conducted inquiries. Such "experiences" are not experiences with doing science.

Learning by experience in some matters is also a dangerous way to go. It is safer and less expensive, in learning to fly a large airplane, to use a simulator before taking the controls even with a trainer as co-pilot and backup who can override the novice in case of danger.

The danger in some kinds of learning is as much or more to clients as to the learners. In medicine the risks to clients are especially important. In this case it is so important nevertheless that the novices accumulate extensive first-hand experience that the expensive procedure of medical internships under close supervision, followed by residencies with less supervision, is employed to achieve the desired level of proficiency and knowledge. In other professions the risk may be to financial interests or to the hazard of imprisonment, as in the case of the legal profession. Where internships or assistantships are used as a part of the development of competent teachers, the risk is that the pupils or students will learn less or even be misinformed. Yet in this case, as in the health professions, the need for broadened experience accompanied by expert assistance in reflecting upon the experience is paramount if a succession of effective practitioners is to be achieved (Mishoe & Courtenay, 1994).

The dangers and the costs of some types of experience have led to efforts to teach by the use of simulations, as mentioned for aviators. Now that computers and telecommunications technologies have so greatly enhanced the feasibility of complex simulations faithfully repeated time and time again, it is much more likely that a realistic experience base can be developed with this type of instruction.

In Chapter 3 we told about UMUC's nuclear science program for operators of nuclear power plants. Not only are the operators and the public at risk if the education of these operators is deficient. The university could be legally liable if its instructional services are not sound.

An interesting complication with "accumulating experience" is the phenomenon of a learner's failure to realize what is happening in the event (Markus, Howard, & King, 1993; Chi, De Leeuw et al., 1994). This phenomenon often occurs with students of anthropology their first time in a foreign culture. The neophyte may well insult a native of that culture without realizing that what was intended as a friendly act or an innocent inquiry has given offense. In a somewhat different sense an expert coach in football or tennis will "see" things the trainee is doing that prevent optimum performance whereas a less expert observer would see nothing wrong or might fail to imagine a way of acting that would improve the results achieved.

FURTHER OBSTACLES IN BUILDING AN EXPERIENCE BASE

The obstacles to building a superior experience base were illustrated above in terms primarily of explicit learning, learning in which the knowledge content can be articulated readily and in which it is natural to reflect upon the experiences and draw inferences from them. Recent research indicates that the sheer quantity of experience also has an impact on how much and what is learned (Ericsson & Lehmann, 1996). For example, research comparing the ways in which experts and novices approach a problem attributes much of the difference in performance to differences in the quantity of experience undergone. Ericsson and Hastie (1994) state:

"The most commonly recognized predictor of competency in a specific type of activity is the amount of experience with that particular activity" (p. 63). This finding has held with chess players, surgeons, teachers, managers, and sales agents (Chi, Glaser et al., 1988).

Even though expertise in such callings is demonstrable in results achieved and in the speed and effectiveness with which problems in the calling are solved, the experts may be unable to articulate what they know. As Reber (1993) reports, experts do not know what they know! Studies comparing what expert gamblers think they do to win and what they actually do disclose significant discrepancies between the two (Coleman, 1976). Expert welders carry out their work differently than they articulate in training syllabi or in feedback during instruction of their novice trainees or interns (Evans & Butler, 1992).

What is it, then, that this build-up of experience does? It seems to contribute to the development of "a feel for," or "an intuition of," the situation and the ability to make "shortcuts" in solving problems. Reber (1993) analyzed more than 40 empirical studies that document the effects of implicit learning upon the development of tacit knowledge. Most human learning, according to Reber, is implicit. "The acquisition of [tacit] knowledge takes place largely independently of conscious attempts to learn and largely in the absence of explicit knowledge about what was acquired" (p. 5). This fact may help explain why it is so difficult for researchers to find out what experts know and how they came to know it. Yet coaches do teach knowledge and skills by a regimen of practice that may not include articulating what is to be learned.

Experience also enhances problem-solving skills (Sternberg, 1986). The highly experienced person finds solutions more quickly, pays attention to aspects of a problem that novices do not, and comes up with more effective solutions than do novices (Chi, Glaser, & Farr, 1988). Hunt (1994) found in a review of research that experts facing a problem pull from memory of earlier experiences a set of problem-solving rules that worked in similar, prior situations. They then short-cut the search and try out the earlier effective ways. If the first try does not work, they search their experience for alternatives (Klein 1997). Less experienced practitioners are likely to try the first solution that comes to mind, one that is based on no experience of actually solving a similar problem (Legrow & Sheckley, 2000). Similar findings are reported by Watson and Johnson-Laird (1972).

Wilson and Lyons (1961) compared eighteen cooperative education colleges with matched non-coop-education ones and found comparable mastery of explicit knowledge but earlier maturation among co-op students. Coleman (1976) identified three features of instruction that are often lacking in classroom studies that are found in "experience-rich" instruction. The latter (a) enlarges both the diversity and the quantity of experience base for reflection, (b) draws on the natural and primary interests of the learner; and (c) uses unexpected elements of experiences as triggers for questioning previously held ideas.

Applying Principle 5: Reflecting Effectively upon the Experience Base

At the beginning of this chapter we described the strategy of alternating work and study periods as a way of both broadening experience and promoting active reflection upon it. Two other major strategies have been developed recently that foster this interplay. One is exemplified by the studio-based physics course at Rensselaer Polytechnic Institute (RPI) and the other in the online courses of University of Maryland University College (UMUC).

The RPI physics course is made possible by developments in instructional technology. The introductory physics course in large universities has traditionally been for students an "experience of sitting in large non-interactive lectures with a lecturer who is statistically unapproachable even when personally approachable"(Wilson, Redish, & McDaniel, 1992). Traditionally 600 to 1000 RPI students per semester enrolled in the introductory courses in physics, calculus, and chemistry. The courses were usually divided into two lecture sections of 300 to 500 students each, and then broken into 25 to 30 recitation sections and 30 to 40 lab sections of less than 25 each. A mix of faculty and teaching assistants staffed this array.

In the spring of 1993 RPI gathered a group of experts to redesign the course. Contact hours were reduced from six per week (two of lecture, two recitation, and two lab) to four (two 2-hour periods or two 1.5-hour periods plus one 1-hour), thus lowering staff costs sharply. Facilities were re-designed to have one studio classroom for up to 64 students and a second for about 50, with 6-foot worktables for two students each, with computer workstations and open workspace, and with space for equipment for the day's hands-on lab. In this arrangement, the instructor could see all workstation screens from the center of the room's oval, and students could turn away from the center of the room to focus on their own group's workspace.

This setup also allowed the instructor to move easily from lecturing about a principle, to having students discuss the principle, to assigning a computer task in which students experiment with the principle, to asking students to discuss their results with their neighbors, or to having students describe their results to the whole class.

The instructional design changed the courses from a largely passive experience for students to one of diverse kinds of activity, including hands-on experience and sophisticated simulations as well as periodic student-to-instructor interaction. A typical session began with discussion of a required homework assignment in which students presented their solutions and drew comments. The instructor then presented a topic for follow-up study in the laboratory. The problem presented might make use of a video-camera focused on a movement that is photographed and digitized for use in each work area. Students analyzed and graphed the motion in varied formats. The students had access to a variety of sophisticated supports developed collaboratively by a consortium of schools.

Research on the RPI studio courses documented enhanced student satisfaction, substantial learning gains over those of the course as earlier taught, and significant reduction of costs. Of particular interest was the fact that the broadening of experience base as well as the heightened reflection was achieved within face-to-face classroom settings.

The UMUC development of online courses seeks to achieve active student-to-student, as well as instructor-student, interaction in ways that deepen the probing of issues and draw on the diverse experiences of the students and the instructor. An excerpt from faculty discussions of this work follows.

The Center for Teaching, Learning & Assessment at UMUC currently enlists a different volunteer faculty member every fortnight to kick off and facilitate a discussion among faculty on some issue about instruction. The forum is known as Factalk.

Recently the issue adopted was that of increasing the level of interaction among students online. Almost at once a faculty member questioned whether mere quantity of interaction was desirable and suggested that instructors would need to intervene to advance the rigor and complexity of analysis elicited in these exchanges. The question precipitated considerable disagreement at first, even about whether to bother with student-student interaction.

Then experienced online teachers began to contribute reports of ways they had found to raise the quality of interactions. Distinctions were introduced between interactions in chat rooms, in conferences within an online course, in study groups within a course, and in completing assignments as contrasted with thinking through an issue for learning's sake.

Some instructors reported problems encountered (e.g., students who did not respond to another student's idea expressed in Week 1 until the last week of the course) and solutions devised (e.g., requiring that every classmate respond "in depth" within four days). It was pointed out that discussion aimed at getting straight on accepted facts was usually a less instructive activity than defending an opinion on an issue for which there is "no right or wrong answer"—a judgment call.

Interwoven through the exchange among faculty online were questions about the writing standards that should be enforced with respect to these interacting messages among students: could the University standards for acceptable writing be relaxed with regard to chat room conversations and study group deliberations, or were those standards to be enforced by grading of all of these types of communication?

Emerging from this kind of exchange are research studies on the ways in which active reflection upon experience deepens learning and can be applied by faculty in online courses to improve the instruction. Preliminary studies at the UMUC raised the question whether instructors in online courses were spending more time interacting with students than in their face-to-face classes and suggested that some students who never got "air time" in class were participating in the on-line interchanges. The question then arose whether some of the work load for instructors could be alleviated and instruction further improved by the instructors' delegating some responsibility for the quality of student-student interaction to some of the students.

While Factalk *discussions have raised traditional concerns about educational quality (knowledgeability of the professor, efforts to create a sense of community, professor's responsiveness to students) it was nevertheless reported that professors "don't have to stay up until all hours answering e-mail:" one teacher responded to only about one in ten messages, enough to let students know he was paying attention, but without creating an impossible workload for himself. Better, however, was the sharing among professors of the many ways they have found, not only to reduce their load, but also to elicit more probing and complex analysis of issues among students in their interactions.*

The Factalk *discussion as a whole, moreover, highlighted how important it is not to leave the amount and depth of reflection to chance, but to employ a variety of means in raising the level of sophistication of the interchange.*

BEING AN ACTIVE LEARNER? WHAT KINDS OF ACTIVITIES?

Whether in face-to-face classes or online courses, teachers can help students benefit from efforts at reflection by following three admonitions:

1. Encourage learners to question others' interpretations of a body of experience, to provide reasons for the questioning, to show an understanding of the others' experiences, and to explain their assumptions about the experiences (King & Kitchener, 1994).
2. Build opportunities for collaborative learning: for participation by the learner in groups that share perspectives, questions, alternative explanations of experience, and different ways of "reading" situations (Ellis, 1994; Springer, Stanne & Donovan, 1997).
3. In making learning active, emphasize the types of activity that are most productive of new learning: exploring alternatives, questioning assumptions, comparing current with earlier problems, checking one's own and others' inference-making for validity, monitoring the credentials of authorities relied upon, caucusing with others on these matters, engaging in well-designed research, using case analyses, and using help in debriefing on own experience (Brookfield, 1987).

Numerous books on learning in college emphasize that more of importance is learned and is longer retained if the learning is active (e.g., McKeachie et al, 1994; Meyers & Jones, 1993). But a close look at examples cited indicates that not just any and every kind of activity has these good effects. So what kinds of activity make the difference? The third of the ways of encouraging reflection mentioned above points to activities that make reflection most effective.

One of the most productive forms of active conduct in learning is that of exploring alternatives to the first idea presented in trying to explain or interpret new experiences or to solve a problem (Gentner & Holyoak, 1997). Experts can short cut lengthy exploration because they have "done it" earlier and can actively search that experience base for alternative interpretations (Holyoak & Thagard, 1997). If presented with a "yes-or-no" choice in decision-making, the learners are less likely to find an optimal option than if they are encouraged to explore diverse notions. The restricted yes-no option may also result in briefer and more superficial consideration of a problem.

A second form of activity that tends to result often in fundamental re-thinking of a proposed conclusion is that of questioning assumptions. Some scholars of instruction (e.g., Brookfield, 1987) regard the ability to recognize unstated assumptions essential to the validity of an argument as the most important to stress in teaching. Often such assumptions are the only part of an argument that is challengeable and are the part that causes its protagonists to come to a false conclusion (e.g., it is easy to assume that an insult was intentional when in fact it may have been inadvertent; or a technician receiving a signal of an incoming missile may mistake it for "the real thing" when in fact the monitoring software has given a false signal). While some critics of adult educators focus on political or sociological assumptions that even their users fail to recognize (e.g., sexist attitudes or ethnic or nationalistic biases) (Brookfield, 1987), these unnoticed sources of misjudgment abound throughout human discourse.

As noted earlier in this book, one of the skills experts have is a habit of an active learner; viz., comparing a current problem with other problems encountered earlier (Ertmer & Newby, 1996; Klein, 1997). The inexperienced learner lacks a problem-bank from which to draw in such comparative reflection. But accumulating experience can be done without the learner's developing the habit of consulting it for alternatives and particularly for lessons learned from earlier successes and failures.

An obvious fourth form of active learning is that of reviewing the pattern of inference-making others have used or the learner has used in arriving at conclusions (Holyoak & Thagard, 1997). Entire sequences of courses are meant to develop the skill to reason validly, especially in complex matters (e.g., in a legal brief argued before the Supreme Court or in the advocacy for a change of public policy on, say, protection of endangered species or the problem of global warming).

Many people reach a conclusion by adopting the ideas of "an authority." But authorities disagree with one another, and not every authority has sound credentials. A useful activity in learning is that of evaluating authorities before acting upon their counsel. It follows that learning early how to evaluate the credentials of authorities can then add a useful form of activity to one's reflective tool kit (Perry, 1970, 1981).

Caucusing with others is another productive way to reflect upon ideas and experiences. By pooling ideas a group of novices can sometimes approximate the breadth of considerations an expert brings to bear on a problem (Ellis, 1994). The literature on collaborative learning is extensive (Blaye, Light, Joiner, & Sheldon, 1991; McKeachie et al., 1994). The case study in Chapter 3 on supplemental instruction at the University of Missouri-Kansas City on "high-risk courses", illustrates use of peer mentors and fellow students to overcome difficulty with the ideas of a mathematics course. The Rensselaer Polytechnic Institute studio course in physics, student conferencing on the Internet, and the UMUC *Factalk* suggestions (all discussed earlier in this chapter) illustrate ways to combine collaborative learning with other active learning tactics to improve results. Some advocates even view peer collaboration in learning as the most productive of study strategies for some students.

Engaging actively in research can be a powerful learning activity. In the graduate program at the University of Connecticut (see case study in Chapter 2) learners conduct semester-long research projects in which they develop their own theory about the topic they are studying (e.g., how experience enhances learning). Throughout the course, learners compare the data they have gathered on a topic with the information published in research journals. In reflective dialogues, learners discuss why their results did or did not match those reported by other researchers. Through this process individuals learn first hand how reflection and experience interact to produce new knowledge.

Case analysis is another way reflection can be used to enhance learning. Oftentimes researchers refer to experts as using "case-based reasoning" (Alvarez, Binkley, Bivens, Highers, Poole, & Walker, 1990; Bradburn, 1993). By this expression they mean that experts frequently use past experiences (cases) to reason about and solve new problems. In so doing, the experts find similarities between a current situation and one in which they achieved a successful resolution in the past. To develop this skill among novices, many institutions guide students through the analysis of actual cases that illustrate key issues and ideas. The best of these programs de-emphasize memorization or recitation of facts about the cases reviewed. It is crucial to avoid overgeneralizing from one or a few cases or overlooking more representative evidence from other studies. Instead, the programs strive to develop learners' abilities to use acquired knowledge from past experiences to inform the resolution of current dilemmas (Barrows, 1994; Evensen, 2000).

Debriefing on previous experience can enable a person to make explicit knowledge that had been unrecognized or tacit. As described briefly at the opening of this chapter, in a case study on management studies Legrow and Sheckley (2000) describe the utility of a prior learning assessment course that required students with considerable prior management experience to articulate what they learned from their prior experiences. When these managers were asked to talk aloud as they solved management problems, their answers were more complex and addressed more key points of the problem scenario than did a group of managers with similar levels of experience who had not participated in the portfolio-development course. More often than not, debriefing (as the term itself suggests) is more productive when another person questions the learner about the earlier experiences and "draws out" or "elicits" the "lessons" (Chi, De Leeuw et al., 1994). Those who have experienced such debriefing often say that they "had not really learned it" until they were obliged to explain themselves to their debriefer.

Reflecting upon previously unrealized learning is but one of a variety of "metacognitive activities" that can yield learning not achievable by other methods (Ertmer and Newby, 1996). Engaging in valid inference making is not itself, as we use terms, a metacognitive activity; but reflecting upon how one goes about inference making correctly or incorrectly and trying to shape further critical thinking efforts with the clarity thus obtained *is* a metacognitive activity (Schraw, 1998). Metacognition is reflecting upon one's own lower order cognitive activities. Memorizing is not a metacognitive activity, but consciously trying to reflect upon one's habits of memorizing and to improve them *is* an instance of metacognition. One might think of metacognition as one's self-policing and re-shaping of one's normal cognitive activities.

To conclude this brief review of ways to engage in active reflection, we have observed that while some forms of mental activity are relatively unproductive, there are numerous ways that can indeed enhance and embed significant learning. Building a habit of metacognition to monitor one's own use of reflection in these latter ways can save one's time and advance the gains in intellectual strength.

Concluding Note

Nothing is more effective in furthering learning than an astute orchestration of experience—hands-on, simulated, and vicarious—combined with a creative variety of modes of active reflection. If an institution of higher education can build patterns of this orchestration into its fundamental culture and operation, its instructors will in turn be strengthened in enhancing the learning of students enrolled in programs and courses of study. As a rising tide lifts all boats, so an institutional climate of high expectations for critical reflection combined with experience-broadening requirements will raise the effectiveness of all instruction.

Instructors in turn can serve their students best, not by relying entirely upon the transmission of a heritage of abstract knowledge, but by drawing on that heritage to lead students into a process of transforming the yield of their own experiences and reflection into a more complex understanding of themselves and their world.

REFERENCES

Alvarex, M. C., Binkley, E., Bivens, J., Highers, P., Poole, C., & Walker, P. (1990). Case-based instruction and learning: An interdisciplinary project. Paper presented at the 34th Annual Conference of the College Reading Association, Nashville.

Astin, A. W. (1962). "Productivity" of undergraduate institutions. *Science, 36:* 129-135.

Barrows, H. S. (1994). *Practice-based learning: Problem-based learning applied to medical education.* Springfield, IL: Southern Illinois University School of Medicine.

Blaye, A., Light, P., Joiner, R., & Sheldon, S. (1991). Collaboration as a facilitator of planning and problem solving on a computer based task. *British Journal of Developmental Psychology, 94:* (2) 471-483.

Bradburn, C. (1993). FLORENCE: Synthesis of case-based and model-based reasoning in a nursing care planning system. *Computers in Nursing, 11:* (1) 20-24.

Broadbent, D. E., FitzGerald, P., & Broadbent, M. H. P. (1986). Implicit and explicit knowledge in the control of complex systems. *British Journal of Psychology, 77,* 33-50.

Brookfield, S. D. (1987). *Developing critical thinkers: Challenging adults to explore alternative ways of thinking and acting.* San Francisco: Jossey-Bass.

Chi, M. T. H., Glaser, R. I., & Farr, M. (1998). *The Nature of experience.* Hillsdale, NJ: Erlbaum.

Chi, M. T. H., De Leeuw, N., Chiu, M., LaVancher, C. (1994). Eliciting self-explanations improves understanding. *Cognitive Science 18:* 439-477.

Clark, B. R. (1970). *The distinctive college: Swarthmore, Reed, Antioch.* Chicago: Aldine Publishing Company.

Coleman, J. (1976). Differences between experiential and classroom learning. In M. T. Keeton & Associates (Eds.): *Experiential learning: Rationale, characteristics, and assessment.* San Francisco: Jossey-Bass.

Conrad, D. & Hedin, D. (1991). School-based community service: What we know from research and theory. *Phi Delta Kappan, 72:* (10) 743-751.

Cubeta, J., Travers, N., & Sheckley, B. G. (2001). Predicting academic success of adults from diverse populations. *Journal of College Student Retention: Research, Theory, & Practice, 2:* (4) 297-313.

Damasio, A. (1999). *The feeling of what happens: Body and emotion in the making of consciousness.* New York: Harcourt Brace & Company.

Edelman, G. M., & Tononi, G. (2000). *A universe of consciousness: How matter becomes imagination.* New York: Basic Books.

Ellis, S., & Siegler, R. S. (1994). Development of problem solving. In R. J. Sternberg (Ed.): *Thinking and Problem Solving.* New Haven, CT: Yale University Press.

Ericcson, K. A., & Hastie, R. (1994). Contemporary approaches to the study of thinking and problem solving. In R. J. Sternberg (Ed.): *Thinking and problem solving* (pp. 37-79). New Haven, CT: Yale.

Ericsson, K. A., Krampe, R., & Tesch-Romer, C. (1993). The role of deliberate practice in the acquisition of expert performance. *Psychological Review, 100:* (3) 363-406.

Ertmer, P. G. & Newby, T. J. (1996). The expert learner: Strategic, self-regulated, and reflective. *Instructional Science, 24,* 1-24.

Evans, G. & Butler, J. (1992). Expert models and feedback processes in developing competence in industrial trade areas. *Training research conducted in higher education.*

Evensen, D. H. (Ed.). (2000). Problem-based learning: *A research perspective on learning interactions.* Mahwah, NJ: Lawrence Erlbaum Associates, Inc.

Gentner, D., & Holyoak, K. J. (1997). Reasoning and learning by analogy: Introduction. *American Psychologist, 52,* 32-34.

Holyoak, K. J., & Thagard, P. (1997). The analogical mind. *American Psychologist, 52:* (1) 35-44.

Hunt, E. (1994). Problem solving. In R. J. Sternberg (Ed.): *Thinking and problem solving.* (pp. 215-232). New Haven, CT: Yale.

Jacobs, Phillip E. (1956). *Changing values in college: An exploratory study of the impact of general education in social sciences on the values of American students.* New Haven, CT: Edward W. Hazen Foundation.

Keeton, M. T. (1977). Credentials for the learning society. In M. T. Keeton (Ed.), *Experiential Learning: Rationale, Characteristics, Assessment.* San Francisco: Jossey-Bass.

King, P. M. & Kitchener, K. S. (1994). *Developing reflective judgment.* San Francisco: Jossey-Bass.

Kitchener, K. S. & King, P. M. (1981). Reflective judgment: Concepts of justification and their relationship to age and education. *Journal of Applied Developmental Psychology, 2,* 89-116.

Klein, G. (1997). The Recognition-Primed Decision (RPD) Model: Looking back, looking forward. In C. E. Zsambok & G. Klein (Eds.): *Naturalistic decision making.* Mahwah: Lawrence Erlbaum Associates.

Kolb, D. A. (1984). *Experiential learning: Experiences as the source of learning and development.* Englewood Cliffs: Prentice-Hall.

Knapp, R. H. & Goodrich, H. B. (1952). *Origins of American scientists: A study made under the direction of a Committee of the Faculty of Wesleyan University.* Chicago: The University of Chicago Press.

Knapp, R. H. & Greenbaum, J. J. (1953). *The younger American scholar: His collegiate origins.* Chicago: University of Chicago Press.

Laurillard, D. (1993). *Rethinking university teaching: A framework for the effective use of educational technology.* London and New York: Routledge.

Legrow, M. & Sheckley, B. G. (2000). Educational benefits of completing a portfolio of prior learning. Paper presented at the International Conference of the Council for Adult and Experiential Learning, Chicago, Illinois.

McKeachie, W. J., Chamm, N., Menges, R., Svinicki, M. & Weinstein, C. E. (1994). *Teaching tips: Strategies, research, and theory for college and university teachers.* Ninth Edition. Lexington, MA: D. C. Heath & Company.

Markus, G. B., Howard, J. P. F., & King, D. C. (1993). Integrating community service and classroom instruction enhances learning: Results from an experiment. *Educational Evaluation and Policy Analysis, 15:* (4) 410-419.

Meyers, C. & Jones, T. B. (1993). *Promoting active learning: Strategies for the college classroom* (pp. 165-171). San Francisco: Jossey-Bass.

Mishoe, S. C. & Courtenay, B. C. (1994). Critical Thinking in Respiratory Care Practice. Paper presented at the 35th Annual Adult Education Research Conference, Knoxville, TN.

Perry, W. G., Jr. (1970). *Forms of intellectual and ethical development in the college years: A scheme.* New York: Holt, Rinehart, and Winston.

Perry, W. G., Jr. (1981). Cognitive and ethical growth: The making of meaning. In A. W. Chickering (Ed.), *The modern American college.* San Francisco: Jossey-Bass.

Reber, A. S. (1993). *Implicit learning and tacit knowledge: An essay on the cognitive unconscious.* New York: Oxford University Press.

Schacter, D. L. (1996). *Searching for memory: The brain, the mind, and the past.* New York: Basic Books.

Schraw, G. (1998). On the development of adult metacognition. In M. C. Smith & T. Pourchot (Eds.): *Adult learning and development: Perspectives from educational psychology.* Mahwah: Lawrence Erlbaum Associates.

Sheckley, B. G. & Keeton, M. T. (1997a). Service learning: A theoretical model, *96th Yearbook on Service Learning, Part 1.* National Society for the Study of Education.

Sheckley, B. G., & Keeton, M. T. (1997b). *Improving employee development: Perspectives from research and practice.* Chicago: Council for Adult and Experiential Learning.

Specht, L. B., & Sandlin, P. K. (1991). The differential effects of experiential learning activities and traditional lecture classes in accounting. *Simulation & Gaming, 22:* (2) 196-210.

Springer, L., Stanne, M.E. & Donovan, S. (1997). *Effects of cooperative learning on undergraduates in science, mathematics, engineering, and technology.* Madison, WI: National Institute for Science Education.

Treisman, P. U. (1990) Mathematics achievement among African American undergraduates at the University of California, Berkeley: An evaluation of the mathematics workshop program. *Journal of Negro Education, 59:* (3) 31.

Van Eynde, D. F. & Spencer, R. W. (1988). Lecture versus experiential learning: Their differential effects on long-term memory. *Journal of the Organizational Behavior Teaching Society, 12:* (4) 52-58.

Wason, P. C. & Johnson-Laird, P. N. (1972). *Psychology of reasoning.* Cambridge, MA: Harvard University Press.

Wilson, J. W. & Lyons, E. H. (1961). *Work-study college programs: Appraisal and report of the study of cooperative education.* New York, NY: Harper & Row.

Wilson, J. (1994). The CUPLE physics studio. *The Physics Teacher. 32:* (9) 518-523.

Wilson, J. M., Redish, E. F., & McDaniel, C. K. (1992). The comprehensive unified physics learning environment: Part II. The basis for integrated studies, *Comput. Physics 6:* (3) 282.

Winter, D. G., McClelland, D. C., & Stewart, A. J. (1981). *A new case for the liberal arts.* San Francisco, CA: Jossey-Bass.

CHAPTER 6

Use Genuine Problems to Arouse Motivation and Enhance Learning

In the 1992-1993 academic year the mathematics faculty of Alverno College made a fundamental change in the instructional strategy they used in the developmental mathematics course. Earlier this course was taught by repetitive drill in basic skills, accompanied by class lectures that stated and explained rules. The new method built primarily on having students solve problems in their daily lives followed by discussion of the math concepts involved. The case, initially reported in 1994 by Suzanne Mente and colleagues, is here updated to 1999.

All students in this study had a history of failure in math courses in which faculty used traditional lecture-based approaches to teaching math. In contrast to the overall college population (20% non-white), the sample of students in the remedial math course was disproportionately non-white (32%). Alverno is a women's college; so all of the students in this study were women, averaging 23 years in age.

Agreed on the need for change, the department faculty searched current literature and practices to develop a more appropriate curriculum. They settled on one that used:

- *authentic data centered on problems of great interest to students to discuss math concepts (e.g., problems of demographics, health-related data, and consumer concerns);*
- *notebooks kept by students that contained homework activities;*
- *opportunities for students to explore "the story behind the numbers," including the "hidden" assumptions and biases in information;*
- *a higher amount of interactive group work than in previous years;*
- *a traditional textbook that was used for self-monitored skills practice only when needed;*
- *course content emphasizing that use of math ideas is necessary for societal and individual improvement;*

- a faculty commitment to "do no harm" (i.e., maintain at least the minimum skill outcome expectations of previous years); and
- all four types of learning activities inventoried in Kolb's work (e.g., new concrete experiences, reflective observation on them, formulation of abstract concepts based on the reflections, and active experimentation using the concepts).

During 1991-1992 the faculty conducted a two semester pilot study in which they assessed the effectiveness of the new math curriculum. Data from two "experimental" sections (student performance, student reactions, and instructors' observations) were compared with similar information from 15 sections that were taught using traditional methods.

Results of the Pilot Study indicated that the revised course was more effective in helping students to learn math in terms of meeting or exceeding scores on traditional tests as well as doing well on new types of tests involving application of math concepts to solve current problems. The pilot group (n = 40) had an average success rate of 89% compared with 75% for the average rate of the traditional classes (n = 376). The most dramatic improvements occurred among Black, Hispanic, Asian, Pacific Islander, and American-Indian students—especially those in the pre-college program. Qualitative changes for the pilot group included more active use of math outside of class, lowering of anxiety about math (more risk-taking in class and in outside use), more asking of math questions of their own, and pride in successes in using math outside of class.

The course continues to be updated and revised following the problem-based curriculum as described. Reported success rates have been consistent through 1999. Subsequent General Education mathematics courses have been revised to follow the philosophy of the more successful pilot course.

Not only was the effectiveness of instruction improved through this innovation, but a number of key costs were also reduced.

- A high proportion of students with a history of failure had success.
- Program completers succeeded in later regular math courses.
- Completers were less inclined to avoid majors that required math.
- Confidence gained carried over to other courses.
- Students increased their participation in class discussions, took more risks in using math concepts, and initiated more questions.
- The number of students retaking the same math course was reduced.
- Improved student success also raised faculty morale and satisfaction.
- Student retention/persistence improved.
- Teachers learned to teach better.
- The costs of repeating the course in later years were reduced.

The college incurred costs in making and evaluating the change. Investment was required in literature study and faculty deliberations in designing the *changed curriculum, in finding and creating materials for it, and in doing the first-time implementation. There were added costs of record-keeping and evaluation in comparing old and new methods. (Mente, 1999).*

Strategies and Tactics for Using Problem-Based Instruction to Enhance Learning

This Alverno story illustrates that effective improvements in instruction often involve interplay among a number of principles discussed in this book. The Alverno innovation began with early assessment of the participants' skills and the tailoring of activities to match the starting capabilities of each student (Principle 3). The course maintained throughout a pattern of deliberate practice, using frequent assessment and prompt feedback (Principle 2). The choice to draw on common life problems that the students were facing may have been the most effective innovation in its effect upon students' interest and motivation (Principle 6). As indicated by research in the field of neuroanatomy, the brain is most focused and uses its resources most effectively when it is addressing problems that are genuine in that they relate directly to learners' current life situations (Edelman & Tononi, 2000).

This use of common life problems also broadened students' experience using mathematics and in facing new problems (Principle 4). Additionally, as the classes were conducted, the process engaged students in collaborative reflection upon the results of their work (Principle 5). Repeated work on different students' problems made for frequent assessment and feedback (Principle 2). The overall plan of work made for an effective matching of the challenge with the learners' starting points and with support adapted to their current capabilities (Principle 3). Some of these principles had also used in the older skill-focussed strategy; but the newer strategy complemented those methods with a more powerful way of engaging the interests of the students and motivating them to master the ideas in ways that would foster retention and ongoing use.

Focus in this chapter will be on Principle 6:

> *To heighten motivation and enhance learning, link the inquiry to genuine problems or opportunities of high interest to the learners.*

WHY BEGIN WITH PROBLEMS?

There are two key reasons for the productivity of linking inquiry to genuine problems. First, interest on the part of the students is immediate and often intense, thus assuring initial motivation (Evensen, 2000). Second, in encouraging students to solve problems instructors concurrently broaden students' experience while engaging them in reflections that advance the development of their understanding of a particular topic. As research on the development of expertise suggests (Chi, Glaser, & Farr, 1988), when individuals solve problems they acquire, through implicit learning, a large degree of tacit (non-conscious) knowledge that is literally "tangled" within the process of solving the problem (Reber, 1993).

Interest in problem-based learning (PBL) has arisen in part in reaction to the effects of content-laden lectures to large enrollment classes in science courses (Barrows, 1994). Because students find such classes "boring" and have difficulty learning information presented in this way, these lecture-based forums have the unintended effect of driving students away from majoring in the sciences. Harold B. White III (1996) states that PBL addresses many of these concerns. In particular, he says that PBL encourages students to take charge of their education, emphasizes critical thinking skills, enhances understanding of course materials, helps students learn how to learn, and improves students' skills in working cooperatively with others.

USING PROBLEMS TO ENHANCE LEARNING

Teachers have developed a variety of ways to foster students' learning through first-hand experience of solving problems (Hmelo, 1998). For example, teachers may:

- Learn about the student's current or earlier problems and find ways to make use of those actual or similar problems for current study tasks;
- Where feasible, pose current learning tasks as ones of problem-solving, not merely accumulation of information;
- With learners who have previous work experience or who are currently employed, draw actively upon their work life as a source of problems for diagnosis and reflection;
- With respect to earlier experience with problems, ask learners to explain why certain attempts did—and other attempts did not—lead to resolution of the problem;
- In fields of study requiring licensure to practice, define key problems learners will encounter in practice and engage them in inquiry focused on coping with those problems, as exemplified in the Keystone Junior College child-care program.

The ways of building into a course of study such opportunities are numerous: internships, service-learning, cooperative education, in-house laboratories, in-class exercises, role-playing, and simulations, as illustrated in the IRAHE case studies cited earlier.

Many adults currently in management positions can benefit from concurrently being enrolled in courses that emphasize critique of current practices or even, at graduate level, conceiving, designing, and initiating new enterprises. Such concurrent broadening of experience while studying has been the tradition in archeology. Today's digs are often nearby in the United States rather than entirely in distant lands and foreign cultures. In archaeology as in anthropology students often need the immediate help of more expert observers in understanding what is being uncovered or experienced, in understanding the importance of preserving a precise record of the location of artifacts found, and in learning how to consider alternative interpretations of the artifacts uncovered. The use of experience-broadening internships is considered a mandatory component of quality programs in fields such as clinical psychology, medicine, nursing, education, and allied health (Allen, Szollos, & Williams, 1986; Krause & Allen, 1988).

MISCUES IN THE USE OF HANDS-ON PROBLEM SOLVING

A common misuse of experience-enriched instruction is postponing the first-hand experience until after "theoretical instruction" has been largely completed, as in legal education and even teacher education (Keeton, 1976; Legrow & Sheckley, 2000). This practice is contrary to findings in the field of neuroanatomy that "doing precedes understanding" (Edelman & Tononi, 2000).

More common today in teacher education is the practice of introducing practica in classrooms over the years rather than just at the end in the senior year. Students can then engage in more advanced levels of responsibility and diversity of teaching contexts as their education continues. Numerous adults in their 40s or later change into teaching from other occupations (e.g., the military services or corporate management) and continue their studies while already teaching or use an interim period between the old and the new occupation to upgrade their preparation (U.S. Department of Education, 1993; Fullan, 1993). By bachelor's completion students with an early experiential start are far more sophisticated in their callings than are those whose hands-on experience has been delayed. Oddly enough, many business schools have similarly eschewed provision of opportunities for practice until *after* the undergraduate years, with a major accrediting body (AACSB) at one time frowning upon any earlier introduction of such opportunities.

A weakness of traditional "summer employment" of students is that they are not supervised either in the workplace or in the college by anyone who discusses and reflects with them on what they are experiencing (Principle 5). Research on service learning (Sheckley & Keeton, 1997b) has documented the greater effectiveness of programs that build regular debriefing sessions into the service period rather than waiting until the very end before beginning the active questioning of what to make of the day-to-day experiences in the service activity.

Ward (1997) describes the important role of structured instruction and debriefing in experiential, service learning activities. At Simmons College many students participate in community service programs that are student-initiated, are short term, require minimum prior preparation, and provide limited opportunities for reflection following service delivery. According to Ward (1997) while the service provided is impressive the learning tends to be "unstructured," and, consequently, is usually overshadowed by the focus on providing a service. In contrast to the loosely structured community service program, Ward (1997) describes the many positive learning gains that students achieve in service activities orchestrated through the carefully designed Social Work program at Simmons College. In contrast to participants in the loosely structured service learning program, students in the Social Work program participate in internships that meld field experiences with regular progress meetings. In progress meetings with their internship advisors and field site supervisors, students discuss issues such as cultural differences and how these differences play out in their work. Ward (1997) concludes that

> . . . service learning is compromised when undergraduates, placed in low-income, ethnic-minority communities, are allowed to underplay or ignore cultural differences and power dynamics that are inherent in the helping relationship. Service learning programs that expose students, through prior academic study and reflection, to requisite information relevant to the ethnic communities in which they will serve provide a necessary corrective to existing problematic service learning practices (p. 147).

Many programs using concurrent or alternating work and study serve only selected parts of a student body. In such situations the sharing of experience among students about their work experiences is not as extensive as among those in which everyone is required either to alternate periods of work with study or to be engaged in both at the same time. Active sharing of problems at work is an antidote to overgeneralization from individual experiences and is a stimulus to exploring alternative interpretations of experience.

INSTRUCTOR ROLES IN PROBLEM-BASED LEARNING

In problem-solving within a higher education context, the role of instructor is best exercised as one of coach or mentor rather than one of lecturer or deliverer of information to be memorized (Daloz, 1986). If the educators' purpose is one of developing intellectual skills and habits, the faculty role is surely not one of indoctrinator (Principle 5).

Actual hands-on experience in solving problems is often impractical due to its costliness in time and dollars. The widespread use of computers in instruction, however, brings an opportunity for the use of simulation in problem-based instruction in ways that both sophisticate the simulation and economize on time and money. For example, in medical education, where "problem-based learning" got this much-publicized name (Barrows, 1994), instructors are increasingly using videotape and computer simulations to show students the "presenting symptoms" of an illness or injury. If a close approximation of the realities being studied can be achieved via videotape or computer simulation, learning can be advanced much more effectively and rapidly than otherwise. To implement this strategy faculty need to develop effective simulations while also designing overall strategies for using the simulations economically.

Weakest among the experiential learning strategies in improving problem-solving skills are those in which the focal "experience" is vicarious in that it depicts situations others, not the learner, have encountered. History is a form of vicarious experience because it involves the retelling of stories based on others' experiences. More frequently vicarious experience occurs when students listen to teachers tell stories of their own experiences. Vicarious experience is more likely to have a significant learning effect if it "connects with" students' own experience in some way (Walter & Marks, 1981). In classes that include adult students with experience applying the ideas being studied, opportunities for those adults to discuss links between ideas being studied in class and real-life problems at work *is* stimulating for everyone involved in the learning effort—teachers included. For all its weakness, nevertheless, learning from vicarious experience is much less time-consuming and less costly in financial resources and other risks than is "trying everything out on one's own." Effective teaching is, as a result, an art of finding a relatively efficient mix of direct, simulated, and vicarious experience with an array of reflective practices that glean and construct an optimal learning process (Laurillard, 1993).

EFFECTIVE STRATEGIES IN THE USE OF PROBLEM SOLVING IN TEACHING

What have practitioners learned about how best to facilitate learning by the use of problems as a starting point for learning? A few findings on best practice are included in the discussion that follows.

Use problems that present a modest challenge for the learners. To enhance learning best, the problems students encounter should not be so easy that solutions are obvious by inspection or can be quickly deduced from given information (Rigby, Deci, Patrick, & Ryan, 1992), but also are not so difficult that the lessons to be learned are not readily apparent (Broadbent, FitzGerald, & Broadbent, 1986). The most productive level of challenge will vary widely from group to group and subject to subject. For this reason teachers cannot easily discern what constitutes "high challenge" for a particular student. According to Knefelkamp, Widick, & Parker (1978) students usually characterize topics as "high challenges" if the topic is not personally important to them, is highly abstract, is highly complex, and has many diverse elements. In contrast students tend to characterize topics as "low challenges" if the topic is personally relevant, can be experienced first hand, is relatively simple to comprehend, and has few subtleties or nuances. In an optimal situation, a problem would combine elements of low and high challenge. For example, asking students in an economics course to devise and monitor a financial portfolio that would provide them with financial security would involve them in a task that was personally relevant (lowering the challenge), provided hands-on experiences as the investments fluctuated on a day-to-day basis (lowering the challenge), was somewhat complex (moderate challenge), but had many diverse elements (increasing the challenge).

Limit the scope of the problems initially used so that many different problems can be tackled during the course or program. For example, in a first year medical school program 27 different problems were addressed during the initial year. Each problem involved the presentation of symptoms to a small group of students, followed by their collective efforts to diagnose the cause(s) of the symptoms and to propose a course of treatment. In line with the principle of deliberate practice, the instructors found that the work required to solve the 27 problems developed in the participants the understanding and habits that would help them to make the medical diagnoses accurately.

Do not rely exclusively on the activity of problem-solving in the overall learning strategy. The faculty of the University of Sydney Medical School found that while a focus on problem-solving was the most effective strategy for teaching diagnostic habits, it was not the most effective for fostering the memory of the facts of human anatomy. According to this study combining memorization tactics with tactics for searching appropriate sources of factual material was better for mastering a knowledge of anatomy (University of Sydney, 2000).

An example of difficulties that can occur with an over-reliance upon PBL is reported by White (1996). In this case the instructor, frustrated with the results of lecturing in anthropology class, became enthusiastic in a two-day workshop about the possibilities of PBL and attempted to use it exclusively in one of his courses. He encountered student resistance to the thrust of responsibility upon them and found great difficulties in developing effective problem scenarios for his students. Student resistance arose in part from those expecting to learn by being told "the right answers." Other students, habitually hard-workers, resented the fact that they bore the burden in small problem-solving groups of making up work that less diligent students failed to do or that less bright students were unable to do. The instructor resolved the situation by adopting a more balanced use of PBL and lecture activities in the course.

Use small groups to speed up the learning and to help learners understand the theory underlying the problems they are addressing. In the Wisconsin Emerging Scholars Program the use of groups of 3 and 4 in tackling problems more difficult than those in the homework assignments was very effective in elevating performance, building further interest in calculus, and building student confidence in themselves as mathematicians.

Such groups must be small enough to keep all members active in their work, but not so small as to make the collaboration of minimal benefit. In a history and philosophy of religion course taught by the senior author the groups, focused on understanding the meaning of key doctrines, needed to be larger than the WES calculus teams, but not as large as a typical discussion class led by the professor as chair. As noted by Sheckley & Keeton (1997a), reflective dialogues that occur in small group sessions can help learners "approximate the thinking processes that experts use" (p. 44).

DRAW ON SIMULATIONS AND MODELING ALREADY DEVELOPED

Instructors can easily be discouraged from using simulations and modeling of problems by the large amount of time required to do them well. An increasing body of cases of widely varying complexity can be found via the Internet.

Once students have success with PBL, encourage them to reflect upon the problem-solving processes themselves rather than solely upon learning the answer to an immediate problem. The task of the group becomes one of metacognition—reflecting upon their own thinking habits and learning how to be more effective learners. Researchers exploring outcomes of college for traditional age learners (Pascarella & Terenzini, 1991) and for adults (Donaldson & Graham, 1999) document metacognitive skills as the factor that differentiates best graduates from non-graduates. Similarly, Ertmer & Newby (1996), in their description of "expert learners" indicate that the more proficient learners are able to monitor, regulate, and self-evaluate their own learning efforts. Instructors who use the strategy advocated here—having students reflect on the process of their own learning—can accelerate students' development of an important set of metacognitive skills.

DIFFICULTIES TO BE AVOIDED IN PROBLEM-BASED LEARNING

What have practitioners learned to avoid when using problems as a starting point for learning? A few findings on best practice are included in the discussion that follows.

Avoid placing students at risk. Some skills, by their very nature, cannot be learned using the PBL process. Students who tried to learn how to fly an airplane or to treat a patient with a life-threatening disease using the PBL process would place themselves and others at risk of serious injury. Such skills can be learned by the use of complex simulators or by undergoing internships or residencies under the immediate supervision of an expert in the art. Such instructional efforts may be problem-based but require distinctive tactics of risk containment or risk avoidance.

Avoid giving students problems that are too difficult. Some problems are too hard for students, not simply because of their lack of knowledge, but also because of the complexity or advanced nature of the problem. Such problems can undermine the motivation of the students without instructing them in the theory that was meant to be disclosed (Broadbent et al., 1986).

Avoid an over-reliance on the problem scenario as the source of all information. Many problems require not only creative or valid reasoning for their solution but also knowledge that is specific to the problem at hand (Wiley, 1998). In such cases, learners may need information that is not present in the problem situation itself. Voss and Post (1988) refer to problems in which the solution becomes apparent only as the problem is being solved as "ill-defined" problems. Oftentimes instructors using PBL in medical programs present students with problems that are "ill-defined." The information required to bring definition to and then solve the problem may be found in textbooks on anatomy, by way of searches on the Web, or by consulting resident experts. Students need to learn that they should not try to resolve risk-laden problems without making sure that they have appropriate knowledge that bears on the diagnosis and on the choice of treatment.

Avoid using overly abstract problem scenarios. Oftentimes instructors can more easily invent abstract problems (e.g., numerical problems for calculating returns on investment) than create plausible, realistic problems that illustrate intended lessons in ill-defined and interesting ways (e.g., how to determine the most profitable mix of items to stock in a retail store). Research findings consistently indicate that very little of the learning that is acquired using abstract problem scenarios typically transfers to use in concrete applications in real-world settings (Solomon, 1994). The more optimistic estimates place the transfer rate at about 20% (Ford & Weissbein, 1997). For this reason we suggest that instructors draw upon realistic scenarios from a variety of fields of application when teaching principles or theories that students will use in broad-ranging applications.

Avoid focusing only on a "right" answer. Laboratory sessions for teaching the physical sciences often require students to explore and answer questions for which the answers are well-known. The lab instructor in these situations grades students' performance by whether or not they obtained the textbook answers. Students' skills in setting up their experiments, in laboratory techniques, in analyzing the sources of variation that may have influenced the results, or in conceiving and accomplishing follow-up studies are seldom assessed. Having students solve only cook-book "problems" may teach them unintended notions about science and scientists. Focusing only on problems with a "right" answer does not teach how scientists actually do science.

Concluding Note

Research in the field of neuroanatomy indicates that experiences in which learners solve genuine problems are of greatest interest and are the most likely to be remembered (Edelman & Tononi, 2000). Only recently has research begun to disclose the considerable role of such experience in the development of expertise (Posner,

1988). The growing numbers of adult learners in college classrooms—with their high interest in the integration of classroom learning with application in the world of practice (Donaldson & Graham, 1999)—can be expected to further efforts to make fuller use of Principle 6. Among the means of improving instruction the ones giving more active attention to linking worksite learning with collegiate instruction and using online simulation of complex problems are likely to be especially effective.

REFERENCES

Allen, G. J., Szollos, S. J., & Williams, B. E. (1986). Doctoral students' comparative evaluations of best and worst psychotherapy supervision. *Professional Psychology: Research and Practice, 17*, 91-99.

Barrows, H. S. (1994). *Practice-based learning: Problem-based learning applied to medical education.* Springfield, IL: Southern Illinois University School of Medicine.

Broadbent, D. E., FitzGerald, P., & Broadbent, M. H. P. (1986). Implicit and explicit knowledge in the control of complex systems. *British Journal of Psychology, 77*, 33-50.

Chi, M. T. H., Glaser, R., & Farr, M. J. (Eds.) (1988). *The nature of expertise.* Hillsdale, NJ: Lawrence Erlbaum Associates, Publishers.

Daloz, L. A. (1986). *Effective teaching and mentoring: Realizing the transformational power of adult learning experiences.* San Francisco: Jossey-Bass.

Donaldson, J. & Graham, S. (1999). A model for college outcomes for adults. *Adult Education Quarterly, 50*(1), 24-40.

Edelman, G. M. & Tononi, G. (2000). *A universe of consciousness: How matter becomes imagination.* New York: Basic Books.

Ertmer, P. G. & Newby, T. J. (1996). The expert learner: Strategic, self-regulated, and reflective. *Instructional Science, 24*, 1-24.

Evensen, D. H. (Ed.). (2000). *Problem-based learning: A research perspective on learning interactions.* Mahwah, NJ: Lawrence Erlbaum Associates, Inc.

Ford, J. K. & Weissbein, D. A. (1997). Transfer of training: An updated review and analysis. *Performance Improvement Quarterly, 10*: (2), 22-41.

Fullan, M. (1993). *Change forces: Probing the depths of educational reform.* Bristol, PA: Falmer Press.

Hendry, G. D. & Wahba, T. (2000). Developing a student-centered approach to evaluation in a problem-based medical course. *Proceedings of the Inernational Conference on the Improvement of Learning and Teaching.* Sydney, Australia.

Hmelo, C. E. (1998). Cognitive consequences of problem-based learning for the early development of medical expertise. *Teaching and Learning in Medicine, 10*: (2), 92-100.

Keeton, M. T. (Ed.) (1976). *Experiential learning: Rationale, characteristics, and assessment.* San Francisco: Jossey-Bass.

Knefelkamp, L., Widick, C., & Parker, C. (1978). *Applying new developmental findings.* San Francisco: Jossey-Bass.

Krause, A. A. & Allen, G. A. (1988). Perceptions of counselor supervision: An examination of Stoltenberg's model from the perspectives of supervisors and supervisees. *Journal of Counseling Psychology, 33,* 77-80.

Laurillard, D. (1993; 1997 Reprint). *Rethinking University Teaching.* New York: Routledge.

Legrow, M., & Sheckley, B. G. (2000). Outcomes of prior vs classroom learning: What are the differences? Paper presented at the International Conference of the Council for Adult and Experiential Learning, Seattle.

Mente, S. (1999). Course innovations in developmental math (Alverno College). In M. T. Keeton (Ed.): *Efficiency in adult higher education: Case studies.* Adelphi, MD: Institute for Research on Adults in Higher Education

Pascarella, E. & Terenzini, P. (1991). *How college affects students: Findings and insights from twenty years of research.* San Francisco: Jossey-Bass.

Posner, M. I. (1988). Introduction: What is it to be an expert? In M. T. Chi, R. Glaser, & M. Farr (Eds.): *The Nature of Expertise.* Hillsdale, NJ: Lawrence Erlbaum Associates.

Reber, A. S. (1993). *Implicit learning and tacit knowledge: An essay on the cognitive unconscious.* New York: Oxford University Press.

Rigby, C. S., Deci, E. L., Patrick, B. C., & Ryan, R. M. (1992). Beyond the intrinsic-extrinsic dichotomy: Self-determination in motivation and learning. *Motivation and Emotion, 16:* (3) 165-185.

Sheckley, B. G., & Keeton, M. T. (1997a). *Improving employee development: Perspectives from research and practice.* Chicago: Council for Adult and Experiential Learning.

Sheckley, B. G., & Keeton, M. T. (1997b). Service learning: A theoretical model. In J. Schine (Ed.): *Service learning: Ninety-sixth yearbook of the National Society for the Study of Education.* Chicago: The University of Chicago Press.

Solomon, I. (1994). Analogical transfer and "functional fixedness" in the classroom. *Journal of Educational Research, 87*(6), 371-377.

U.S. Department of Education (1993). *National excellence: A case for developing America's talent.* Washington, D.C.: U.S. Government Printing Office.

University of Sydney School of Medicine. Paper presented at the International University Conference on Improving Learning and Teaching, 2000. In *Proceedings of the IUCCILT, 2000.* Adelphia, MD: University of Maryland University College.

Voss, J. F., & Post, T. A. (1988). On the solving of ill-structured problems. In M. T. H. Chi, R. Glaser, & M. J. Farr (Eds.): *The Nature of Expertise.* Hillsdale: Lawrence Erlbaum Associates.

Walter, G., & Marks, S. (1981). *Experiential learning and change.* New York: John Wiley & Sons.

Ward, J. (1997). Service learning in a social work program. In J. Schine (Ed.): *Service learning: Ninety-sixth yearbook of the National Society for the Study of Education.* Chicago: University of Chicago Press.

White, H. B. III (1996). Dan tries problem-based learning: A case study. In *To improve the academy, 15,* 75-91. Stillwater, OK: New Foreman Press and the Professional and Organizational Network in Higher Education.

Wiley, J. (1998). Expertise as mental set: The effects of domain knowledge in creative problem solving. *Memory and Cognition, 26:* (4) 716-730

Wilson, J. M. (1997) Studio teaching: When the future becomes the present. *UniServe Science News, 7:* 3-5.

Wilson, J. M. (1994). The CUPLE physics studio. *The Physics Teacher, 32,* 518.

CHAPTER 7

Develop Learners' Effectiveness as Learners

In the mid-1980s the Weatherhead School of Management of Case Western Reserve University surveyed its corporate clients and alumni to procure testimonials that would help the School market itself in a capital campaign. The responses were so disappointing, relative to the high praise the faculty had expected, that the School began a sustained improvement effort. The resulting innovations enabled the School's students (a) to take a more active role in learning principles of management and (b) to develop greater proficiency in applying these principles.

The new Weatherhead program had six key elements: (1) the Managerial Assessment and Development course, (2) a "Learning Plan," (3) core courses, (4) "Executive Action Teams," (5) perspectives courses, and (6) advanced electives (Boyatzis, Cowen, Kolb, & Associates, 1995). Students begin their program of study by clarifying what they intend to learn (their goals). In their initial course, Managerial Assessment and Development, they learn skills that enable them to develop a learning plan that will allow them to assess and continually develop their knowledge and abilities throughout their careers. The course engages students in much more intensive assessment of their skills and feedback on their development than has been typical of their earlier studies. As a result of the assessment-feedback process they become skilled in monitoring and improving their own learning efforts. This capability has then been used in ongoing work on the other elements of the program.

After the initial pilot offerings of the new program, an evaluation of the learning outcomes disclosed that students made significant improvements. The results documented in two studies of graduating students indicated that students made significant gains in their grasp of theory. In addition, students enhanced significantly their skills in information gathering, information analysis, use of quantitative analysis and technology skills, and ability to initiate actions. The results also indicated that students improved their "sense-making" skills. Some abilities were not as well developed as in other types of management programs (e.g., interpersonal abilities). The Weatherhead School has continued its emphasis in this program upon the early development of its students' capabilities as learners.

Learning to Learn

Of all the things one might hope to learn in college or earlier, none is more valuable than becoming a highly effective and efficient learner (Pascarella & Terenzini, 1991). Becoming an effective learner is a major key to lifelong proficiency and to expertise in a person's choice of career. Principle 7 focuses attention on this effort.

> *Principle 7:* **Early and continuing focus on learners' becoming highly effective and efficient in learning can speed up and deepen learning in later work.**

What characterizes a highly effective and efficient learner? Such a learner is one who enjoys learning, clarifies goals early and repeatedly, is persistent, self-reliant, resourceful, and confident in learning and manages the effort well (Ertmer & Newby, 1996). Being an effective and efficient learner requires that an individual can monitor his/her own deliberate practice, knows how to seek help in a strategic and timely fashion, and knows how to access appropriate tools for learning. According to Winne (1997) as well as Zimmerman (1994), self-regulation is a key attribute of individuals who are described as "effective learners."

A college can speed up and enhance students' learning and reduce costs to learners in no better way than by the early development of learners' awareness and skill in monitoring their own ways of learning, a skill called metacognition (Schraw, 1998). While modest gains in learning effectiveness can be achieved by re-designing teaching and providing better resources for teachers (e.g., an infrastructure for distance learning), more radical gains require a combination of instructional improvement with changes in the habits and abilities of the learners (e.g., setting goals, mapping steps in learning, practicing, monitoring progress, and building expertness in learning). Only the learner, after all, can do the learning. To achieve truly expert levels of effectiveness, learners must engage in deliberate practice over about a decade and, to sustain the expertness, must continue practice at a high level (Principles 1 and 2) (Ericsson & Lehmann, 1996).

The material in this chapter complements that of other chapters by clarifying what it requires to be an effective learner and then discussing how educators can help learners become highly effective in their learning. We argue that to develop this proficiency is a key step in the journey to achieving lifelong efficiency in learning. To elaborate on this point we provide additional stories about enhancing students' learning to learn. We then ask what made the changes in their performance possible and how teachers can systematically foster such growth most effectively. We conclude by discussing ways in which a college can provide the culture and the support that enable faculty to elicit learning expertise among their students on an ongoing basis.

Teaching Effectiveness in Learning

Is it possible for instructors, while teaching a history, literature, psychology, or science course to help students simultaneously develop their effectiveness as learners while also learning the content covered in the course? Or are special courses or training needed to focus solely on developing learning effectiveness? The available research, which is not extensive, suggests that skill in learning is best built in the context of dealing with a specific body of other knowledge (Travers & Sheckley, 2000). This research also suggests that integrating the agenda of learning effectiveness with that of becoming knowledgeable in a discipline requires a distinctive strategy, one appropriate to the dual agenda (Ertmer & Newby, 1996).

Skills in learning to learn will not grow as an automatic side-effect of becoming knowledgeable about a single topic area such as history or psychology. Yet the most effective approach to building metacognition (that is, thinking about one's thinking) is to weave this task into the work of accumulating a specific body of knowledge (Winne, 1997). For some teachers specialized in a discipline or profession, this task of melding the learning of specific facts with the development of thinking skills will present a hard change in the course structure. Will coverage of a particular topic (e.g., an analysis of the treaty ending the Civil War) have to be sacrificed in order to teach certain skills (e.g., how to self-evaluate a homework assignment)? To avoid this choice, the authors focus here on weaving together the development of learning effectiveness with other instructional goals included in a course.

Table 7-1 summarizes key strategies for helping students realize a primary goal of college education, achieving proficiency as learners.

Table 7-1. Strategies for Cultivating Proficiency in Learning

1. Build learners' awareness early in their programs about the usefulness of proficiency in learning.

2. Make clear to students the characteristics of highly effective learners.

3. Incorporate into each task of the course or learning activity components that enhance students' effectiveness as learners.

4. Help students learn how to self-monitor their own learning habits and self-evaluate how those habits enhance their proficiency as learners (a metacognitive capability).

5. Assess in pre-course activities and post-course activities students' proficiency as learners.

6. Help students develop skills in using tools such as information technologies in ways that enhance their learning while also saving them time.

Developing Students' Ability as Learners

The description of the Weatherhead School of Management program outlines one of the many different tactics institutions use to apply the strategies outlined in Table 7-1 to evoke students' growth in learning how to learn. In the three case studies of programs at Alverno College (Bowne & Englemann, 1999; Mente, 1999; Witkowski & Magness, 1999), for example, the faculty put great effort into their choice of instructional goals for a course. Their decisions were guided by careful review of the research literature as well as reflections on students' performance. Using this information the faculty incorporated assessments of students' capabilities in key skill areas (e.g., communications skills, comprehension of written materials) at the very outset of instruction. Faculty used these assessments to make students aware of how they could improve.

Using a different tactic, Empire State College (Keeton, 1999) typically assigns each entering student (all are adults) a mentor who works with the student to design a degree contract between the student and the College. This master contract includes a number of subcontracts that must be completed to fulfill state-and-college-mandated requirements for the baccalaureate degree (e.g., a subcontract to study family dysfunctionality as part of a major in psychology). Each subcontract fits at the same time the individual's goals and ways of learning. This process of choosing goals, planning how to meet them, obtaining evaluators to help assess progress on each subcontract, reviewing progress periodically and, if needed, re-planning and re-negotiating the contract is a process that requires students to take increasing responsibility for their learning. Through this process they also develop increasing proficiency in learning how to monitor and plan their own learning.

A kindred strategy is used in other institutions. Instructors of individual courses in many colleges engage their students in setting goals, planning, implementing the plans, and evaluating the outcomes and the route to them, as in the Antioch course reported early in Chapter 2 (pp. 12–13).

A recent book, *Who Teaches? Who Learns?* (Jenkins & Romer, 1998), relates stories from seven liberal arts colleges that have experimented with "student-faculty partnerships" as a vehicle for remedying an almost astonishing absence of students from the discourse on changing the orientation of educational institutions from an "Instructional Paradigm" to a "Learning Paradigm." As we interpret these experiments (e.g., in Pomona College, Furman University, and others), the faculty selected a number of students to serve as co-leaders who planned goals, projects, and procedures for enhancing students' learning. These student leaders in turn engaged other students in the planning process, thus spreading the pattern of learning-to-learn to a larger segment of the college. In each of the cases instructional activities drew upon the learning interests that students had at the outset of a course of study. From this starting point students were encouraged to take responsibility for a choice of goals for each particular learning activity, whether it was to be a course, a workshop, an "independent-study project," a training sequence, a college-wide drive, or a casual inquiry. As a result of taking such responsibility learners gained further skills in the methods of learning and further confidence in themselves as learners. They did so by practice in developing and helping carry out a plan of instruction, then discussing with more experienced instructors what did or did not work, and by evaluating the end results.

In another institution a group of women students wanted to use their quest to run the Boston Marathon together as the focal point for a learning project. They worked with faculty to translate their interest into a specific learning plan. The plan included credits in Physiology of Women (fitness and conditioning), American History (the storied past of the neighborhoods of Boston they would traverse), Urban Sociology (the interplay of the diverse ethnic cultures along the course), English Composition (journals they wrote to chronicle their quest), American Literature (books written by authors who lived along the route), and Marketing (obtaining sponsors to raise money for a local charity). In supporting this effort the faculty focused on enabling the students to become more effective learners as they learned the disciplinary content of their respective courses.

What Does It Take to Be an Effective Learner?

Building on the wide body of research on self-regulation (Winne, 1995a; Winne, 1995b; Zimmerman, 1990; Zimmerman, 1994; Zimmerman, 1995; Zimmerman & Kitsantas, 1997; Zimmerman & Risemberg, 1997; Travers & Sheckley, 2000), we have explored the extent to which teaching students how to learn can lead to changes in the way they approach their studies. According to Travers (1998), becoming an effective learner involves an interplay among many of the factors discussed in this book:

- wanting to learn (i.e., have interests that are very important and are served by the learning activity about to be carried out) (Principle 6);
- getting one's learning goals clear (Principle 1);
- being persistent about the learning (Principle 2);
- relying upon oneself to accomplish the learning (Principle 3);
- being resourceful in getting help with the learning (Principle 3);
- having confidence in oneself as learner; believing that one can learn what s/he sets out to learn (Principle 3);
- managing time in learning well (Principle 3);
- using deliberate practice until use of the learning becomes almost automatic (Principle 2); and
- finding and using methods that organize and support one's learning effort (Principle 1).

Integrating these nine elements of practice into the study activities of a treatment group of adults in community college math courses resulted in interesting and significant differences with a comparison group of adult learners (i.e., learners participating in classes taught by a traditional lecture-discussion method) (Travers, 1998). The results of a path analysis indicated that for students in the comparison group decisions about what to learn and how to learn it were centered on directions provided by the teacher. In contrast, students in the treatment group reported significantly greater control over the decisions they made about their own learning. Where the learners in the control group followed the directions provided by the teacher, students in the treatment group viewed the teacher as only one in a set of resources to use in making decisions about how and what to learn.

Can this set of requisites be organized in a more compact way? Yes. Together they add up to learning how to manage one's own learning. Being such a manager does not, however, mean refraining from use of help from others. Quite the contrary! Good management of one's own learning includes getting more expert help whenever it is needed and it is feasible to do so. Sometimes a learner may need to ask an expert teacher or coach to take the lead in mapping a plan of work for a particular learning effort, but doing so need not mean the learner surrenders responsibility to the teacher.

How to Facilitate Learning to Learn

How then can a teacher best help students become more expert learners? A good first step is helping them to understand what is involved in being a proficient learner as, for example, in Travers' (1998) analysis. As a second step, instructors should engage learners as soon as possible (as in the Alverno examples) in evaluating their own learning (Bowne & Englemann, 1999; Mente, 1999; Witkowski & Magness, 1999). These two steps help learners to build habits in learning effectively, in taking responsibility for self-direction, and in self-monitoring their own learning activities. Through application of these two steps, students learn to apply the principles of learning discussed earlier in this book naturally in their own studies. They learn to: define learning goals clearly, design and adopt a plan for reaching them, use deliberate practice, set high goals, prompt help-seeking as needed, broaden and reflect upon experience in the field of study, and tackle significant problems from which much can be learned.

Students may encounter a surprising amount of difficulty in carrying out these activities. A teacher can quickly "tell" a student what is involved in taking charge of one's own learning, but enabling the student to gain proficiency may require months or years of effort on a student's part. For example, students at the Weatherhead School required two full years to gain this proficiency. Enabling students to be most effective in managing their learning is a matter of helping them build suitable habits while also having them understand that habit-formation is normally a slow process.

In the teaching experiment at Antioch College cited in Chapter 2, one instructor left a third of the students' expected study time free for their use in self-directed learning if they so chose. Self-direction was defined as choosing what to learn, how to learn it, and how to evaluate what was learned. Most students were eager to take the option. On the first task—deciding what to learn—the students, though well above average for college entrants in verbal skills, ran into several difficulties. First, though wanting to make their own choices, not all had a clear idea of what good options there were. Second, after making a first choice, a number changed their minds. Third, after settling on a choice, most found that it was not clearly defined. Fourth, once these hurdles were overcome, few knew enough about resources for learning in this field to make good choices within a reasonable time about how best to meet the learning goals they had chosen. Students were reluctant to ask faculty members for help because oftentimes the students believed that so doing would be giving up their control. Students also struggled with obtaining an unbiased evaluation of their self-directed learning. In spite of these difficulties, these students showed a significant gain in their autonomy as learners in comparison with a set of students who had not attempted to direct their own learning.

SELF-DIRECTION FOR LEARNING

In his book, *Self-Direction for Lifelong Learning: A Comprehensive Guide to Theory and Practice*, Philip Candy (1991) examines in detail the ways in which individuals become autonomous and effective learners. Synthesizing prior research on this topic, Candy (1991, pp. 134-135) states (we paraphrase for brevity) that autonomous learners:

- Diagnose and assess, with or without the help of others, their own learning needs;
- Select appropriate sources of help with learning and, if needed, give up some independence to expedite the learning;
- Develop, by inquiry and reflection, a grasp of criteria for evaluating the learning being undertaken;
- Seek justification for rules, procedures, principles, and assumptions that otherwise might be taken for granted;
- Challenge what others (e.g., teachers or trainers) state or require where the statements or requirements seem critically unacceptable;
- Cultivate and use an awareness of alternative learning strategies, interpretations of information, and value positions to make reasoned choices about routes to follow in achieving goals;
- Review continually the process of learning (as both a cognitive and a social phenomenon), and, to optimize learning, adjust strategies and tactics used;
- Conceive goals, policies, and plans independently of pressures from others;

- Develop an understanding of phenomena so as to be able to explain the phenomena to others in words and under circumstances unlike those in which they were first encountered;
- Form opinions and clarify beliefs independently, yet relinquish such beliefs and alter opinions when relevant contrary evidence is presented regardless of the presence or absence of extraneous rewards or pressures;
- Pursue a learning goal with equal vigor and determination regardless of external factors such as the increase or decrease of rewards for pursuing or attaining the goal;
- Determine what is really of personal value or in their own interest, as distinct from what may be expedient or convenient;
- Be willing and able to see alternative points of view as legitimate and to deal with objections, obstacles, and criticisms of their goals without becoming incapacitated, threatened, or angry; and
- Demonstrate a sober and realistic appraisal of their shortcomings and limitations, tempered by a cautious but positive awareness, based on past experience of their strengths, abilities, and motivations as learners.

As the first bullet above indicates, self-directed study may include expert help and may be more effective when such help is used (Brookfield, 1985; Mezirow, 1985). As Candy (1991) also observes, self-directedness under the guidance of a teacher (as in independent study in college) and autonomous learning outside of an institution [as in the adult learner projects reported by Tough (1979) and others] are different in the demands made on the learner. Malcolm Knowles (1978) gained fame for his advocacy for adults' taking charge of their own learning. Adherents of this ideal have found, however, that many adults want instructors to tell them initially what and how to learn. Many educators of adults have found that changing this mind-set is by no means easy. Yet with persistence and careful instructional designs, instructors can overcome this resistance and encourage adults to manage their own learning. Although some researchers (e.g., Candy, 1991) recommend that instructors be "realistic and cautious" when trying to elicit self-direction, our experience indicates that instructors who are optimistic in their approach to eliciting self-directed learning (estimating a 60% chance of success, say, instead of a realistic 40%) are usually successful.

Learners express self-direction in their learning in many different ways. We therefore do not mean to suggest that all learners must go about learning in the same way; even methods that work best for most students should not be imposed on all (Sheckley, 1984). Travers (1998) argues for a distinction between self-directedness and self-regulation in learning. She sees the ideal of self-directedness as learning without a dependence upon interactions with others. In contrast, the ideal of self-regulation is achieved when learners monitor and evaluate their learning. What, then, can a teacher best do to facilitate students' success in learning how to further their own learning?

How to Help Learners Regulate Their Own Learning

At the outset, instructors can frame their role in terms of helping learners to set goals for each learning activity being undertaken. Most teachers set goals for their students without asking for ideas, contributions, or consent from learners. The teachers may even feel obliged to set the goals because they are told that good teachers do so, their department expects them to set specific goals, or they believe that "the material this course covers" must be mastered to get a license or a certificate the students are assumed to want. In other words, "if you enrolled in this course, you must want what I offer."

Of all the obstacles to teachers' giving students some choice of learning goals, none is probably greater than the belief that "covering the material" is an instructor's fundamental responsibility. The Rensselaer Polytechnic Institute experience with studio delivery of physics courses (Wilson, 1994) suggests that instructors can "cover the material" in a course while also allowing students to take responsibility for their learning. The Weatherhead School's approach also underscores this same point.

In these and other cases, allowing students to take more responsibility for their own learning— being joint choosers with their instructors of the ways to achieve and monitor learning goals— may reduce coverage of certain materials at early stages of a curriculum. Later in the curriculum students' enhanced abilities to direct, monitor, and regulate their own learning will more than make up for the slow start. So a first step toward enabling students to become effective learners is to insist on their taking an ever-increasing part in choosing how to monitor and evaluate their achievement of instructional goals. So doing can also contribute to the students' enjoying the process of learning and taking joy in its pursuit.

At the same time a college or university should itself have clarified its priorities as to the outcomes of student learning. To certify to the public that a student has earned a degree, the institution must have insisted upon some key outcomes (e.g., in a doctoral program that the graduate has demonstrated proficiency in research and has actually made an original contribution to knowledge in the field). If the university has no demands as to the outcomes assured by a given credential, students may opt for outcomes well removed from what the institution has advertised it will elicit. In other words, the choice of outcomes to achieve within collegiate studies is, as suggested above, a joint responsibility in which the autonomy of each stakeholder is respected.

A further aspect of setting goals is for the student to join in setting the level of proficiency and knowledge to be attained in this experience. This step also draws students into taking ownership of the goal. As the Weatherhead faculty stated in helping their M.B.A. students develop, seeing the difference between where one is and where one wants and needs to be is essential to clear goal-setting and self-regulation (Zimmerman, 1990). This difference is the discrepancy to be overcome via the anticipated learning experience.

When first offering a course, teachers often dictate to students the goals for that course but they do not state the minimum acceptable level of attainment they will demand for credit—or a specific letter grade—in the course. They may not be able to decide what this level is until they have further experience with the course. Students who direct and monitor their own learning need not settle for the teacher's evaluative criteria, but can take charge of setting the level higher than the floor that the teacher will demand.

With a goal in mind and an estimate of the discrepancy to be overcome, students need to create a plan of work to get from where they are to where they want to be (Locke & Latham, 1990). Failure of secondary schools to generate students' abilities in self-directedness and self-regulation means that college students' initial attempts to set realistic plans are likely to fail. Practice after reflection on why the first plans did not work can lead to better plans on later attempts. To help students in this task of learning to generate sound plans of work a teacher needs to encourage their help-seeking, including seeking the teacher's own help, and to avoid completely dictating those plans (Krarabenick & Knapp, 1991). An instructor can suggest a set of feasible plans along with information on reasons that different students might do best with different options. As a first step in taking responsibility for their learning, students can then choose the alternative that fits best their own learning goals. As students gain experience in what works for them as learners and what does not, they can hone their skills in working-at-learning (e.g., in mustering tools they use well, in early help-seeking on puzzling steps in the learning, or in knowing how to distinguish sound intellectual resources from unreliable ones).

With goals and plans for learning in hand, students often need help in initiating the processes of assessment of their progress, identifying their sources of error, and in using feedback to entrench their sound ways of thinking and correct their patterns of error. Students need to create a habit of frequent practice and eliciting feedback on each performance, as was discussed in Chapter 2. On computer-scoreable tasks students can be provided keys and coached not to repeat exercises until they think they understand the sources of their errors. (See the North Carolina State story in Chapter 2.) The lesson to be learned is not simply what answers were right or wrong, but why and what processes of thinking led reliably to correct or best answers and what did not.

A common mistake in teaching is to assume that a skill can be achieved by students with a teacher's demonstrating it and the students' undergoing a minimum of practice and of re-trying after feedback from early attempts. "You see, you can do it!" said a teacher after such a demonstration. "I see that you can do it," responded a young woman in the front row. Using demonstrations as an instructional strategy enables students to see that the teacher can use the skill. The strategy, however, does not always help students to learn the demonstrated skill. In a typical class to develop cognitive or other skills, a reduction of half or more in lecturing time (as in the RPI innovation) (Wilson, 1994) and a matching increase in assessment and feedback activity would have a high probability of enhancing learning. An initial investment of time in creating helpful assessment instruments and processes or in borrowing and adapting them from others can eventually save further time for both teachers and students, as the RPI and North Carolina State examples illustrate.

Feedback is largely wasted if it discourages further effort or if it is not followed by re-planning. Normally the feedback will indicate that significant ideas were misunderstood or that needed skills are not yet at high enough levels. If the criticism is felt by the learner as blaming rather than encouragement, the commitment to keep trying may suffer. Effective feedback, by contrast, encourages renewed effort and is often accompanied by re-planning of next steps in learning and sometimes more fundamental revision of course or curriculum design (Kluger & DeNisi, 1996). So learners need to be helped to learn to choose well in such re-planning. (See the discussion of feedback and re-planning in Chapter 2.)

As teachers help students upgrade their ability to manage learning, the students need to learn how to think about their ways of thinking. Learners who do not engage in this effective metacognition are almost sure to continue in their old ways. One of the great services of a coach is to observe with precision what the athlete is doing that enhances or diminishes performance, to make the athlete aware of these observations, and to advise on how to correct the habits that need to be changed. If a mentor or instructor can provide a similar service to a student with regard to the student's ways of learning, the student can develop a further level of ability as an expert learner.

COMPLEMENTING SELF-REGULATION WITH WORK ON ENHANCING ABILITIES

Becoming more effective in managing one's processes of learning can yield still greater efficiency if key abilities such as monitoring one's own cognitive activities and critical thinking are also strengthened (Zimmerman, 1994). If these abilities are among an institution's intended priority outcomes, instruction and assessment should address progress on these ends as much as, or more than, progress on content learning. In the North Carolina State case, instructors followed up the computer feedback on errors and successes with questions to the students about why some of their tactics had worked and others did not. The questions served to deepen the learning of both principles of physics and the extent to which students could succeed on their own.

Pascarella and Terenzini (1991) found that the greatest differences between college freshmen and seniors was not measured in terms of how much they knew but rather in how they thought. Seniors tended to score moderately higher than freshmen on measures such as general verbal skills (d=.56 1), specific subject knowledge (d=.84), and Piagetian (formal) reasoning (d=.33). In contrast seniors scored much higher than freshmen on measures such as critical thinking (d = 1.0), use of reason and evidence to address ill-structured problems (d=1.0), and ability to deal with conceptual complexity (d=1.2). These results are not surprising. Most every college in America professes the goal of helping students improve their critical thinking skills.

In most cases, however, no specific instructor in such a college views himself or herself as responsible for particular contributions to that institutional goal: The faculty may assume that the improvement in critical thinking will emerge in some indirect or automatic way. Very likely, in the light of the research on implicit learning (Broadbent, FitzGerald, & Broadbent, 1986; Reber, 1993), this gain in critical thinking derives from repeated—but not explicitly intended—use of that skill in diverse courses. A college, however, should not leave this outcome entirely to chance. As told in its case study, Antioch College students of the 1950s and 1960s usually showed gains in critical thinking capabilities as a result of students' participation in alternating work and study programs, being required to take responsibility for learning and living tasks, and engagement in inquiry projects. Other strategies of repeated practice of critical inquiry can succeed also. In any event, to help students learn how to learn a college should consider and adopt a strategy for helping students to gain proficiency in learning that is suited to its own goals and those of its students.

Instructors do not often realize that students' early work on enhancing critical thinking skills can in turn improve their later efforts to learn other kinds of skills and to master significant bodies of knowledge. As a consequence within college curricula no specific plans are made or responsibilities assigned for seeing to this early development. The application of these important skills to broader learning can occur only if students learn how to transfer learning-to-learn skills and appreciate the importance of doing so.

Champions of critical thinking are often not fully aware of the many different meanings typically assigned to that label among instructors from different disciplines and observers such as legislators, parents, employers, and the press (Sternberg, 1996). Widely useful skills are those of learning to recognize the differences between valid and invalid inference-making and to improve one's skill in deduction, making useful distinctions of meaning in ambiguous usages, and clarifying the meanings of propositions (Sternberg, 1994). Different skills (but often included among skills called "critical thinking") are the recognition and helpful defining of problems, brainstorming of creative alternatives for attacking a problem, identifying needed but missing information for resolving a problem, and selecting the best of approaches to resolving a problem in the absence of conclusive information (Sternberg, 1997). There is a great difference in difficulty and utility between the ability to solve well-defined problems and the ability to solve ill-defined problems (Voss & Post, 1988).

Students of the sciences, such as RPI's physics students, may learn key elements of critical thinking as applied to a particular field without necessarily transferring the use of those skills to applications in other sciences or other professions (Solomon, 1994). If a college adopts the goal of proficiency in critical thinking across the range of adult roles, a careful choice of strategy is required, one that involves students in much practice in a variety of contexts. For example, as already mentioned, Alverno College (Mente, 1999) does not regard a concept as truly understood unless the student can apply it appropriately in at least three different contexts.

Another service provided by many colleges today, as reported in Chapter 4, has a related side benefit in fostering self-direction in students; viz., the service of assessing what students have learned outside of formal schooling that is comparable to, or equivalent in value to, what is learned in the institution's courses. Many institutions award either academic credit or waivers of course requirements and advanced standing to students who demonstrate knowledge and skill in this way. But a by-product of the courses on how to make and defend the claims of prior knowledge is the mastery of the difference between making a claim and proving it with adequate evidence (Legrow & Sheckley, 2000). Best practice in portfolio-assisted assessment of non-school learning involves training the student to know the difference between claim and evidence and to distinguish the relative merits of different kinds of testimony and different kinds of demonstration of proficiency and knowledge. Where students present products or offer performances to demonstrate their skills and knowledge, some form of debriefing or oral examination on the thinking underlying the performance or the creation of the product is normally needed to disclose the capabilities employed in doing the work.

Institutional Support for Students' Learning to Learn

An institutional culture that calls for students to become expert learners can greatly enhance the effectiveness of individual efforts by faculty members and students. (Chapter 8 discusses this topic in greater detail.) A college with such a culture will seed its literature with declarations of this commitment and with reports and recognition of successes in its implementation. Emphasis on the goal in recruitment literature may attract students with pre-collegiate experience in taking responsibility for their learning, thus gaining a head start on the enhancement the college or university can generate.

A learning-to-learn culture will provide assistance to faculty in their learning how best to implement the strategies sketched earlier in this chapter. An example of such support in Indiana University Purdue University Indianapolis (IUPUI) is reported by Hellyer (1998). The average age of an IUPUI student at the time reported was 27. Students may have come from any of 90 countries. Many students are from the first-generation in their families to attend college. Most attend only part-time in order to work to help pay their costs. The university has created a program called "Network for Excellence in Teaching" that invites competition among faculty for mini-grants (e.g., $6000 for a full-time six-week period of course development) to improve their teaching effectiveness. One such award went to a psychology professor to improve learning in a course in which 47% of enrolled students failed each test. The course, understandably, contributed greatly to dropouts from the university. The new course, focusing heavily on supporting students' learning-how-to-learn, resulted in marked improvement in end-of-course achievement, student satisfaction, and class attendance. With another award a teacher of public affairs altered his course from one focusing on content only to one with explicit focus on using critical thinking skills to learn the content. Pre- and post-test assessments documented statistically significant gains on all skills but one. Students judged the new course more interesting as well as more challenging.

In papers presented to the 23rd UMUC International Conference on Improving University Teaching, McCombs & Lauer (1998) indicate that the current reforms and transformations of educational practices are informed by knowledge about the nature of learning, learner needs, and individual differences among learners. The transformation, they argue, turns on the use of learner-centered practices and policies that have been empirically tested. This change to learner-centeredness requires, according to Barr & Tagg (1995) that institutions change from a mission to instruct to a mission to produce learning by whatever means work best. Efforts to implement this idea in Further Education in Great Britain have led to the observation:

> In learner-centered colleges, students are expected to be responsible for their own learning, but with self-help from expert systems and specialist staff. These colleges also are designed to respond to individual learning plans. . . . The overall strategy is to establish a customer focus, processes for quality improvement, and ongoing staff development. (McCombs & Lauer, 1998)

Achieving Expertise in Learning

Researchers who study expertise and its development report that "individuals do not achieve expert performance by gradually refining and extrapolating the performance they exhibited before starting to practice but instead by restructuring the performance and acquiring new methods and skills" (Ericsson & Charness, 1997, p. 5). Individuals, the researchers continue, "attain an expert level, not merely as an automatic consequence of more experience with an activity but rather through structured learning and effortful adaptation" (Ericsson & Charness, 1997, p. 5).

Empirical research on becoming an expert has been confined to a very limited number of readily replicable kinds of outstanding performance. Advanced learning in more complex professions does not fit these conditions. Nevertheless, the findings of such studies do throw helpful light on the ways in which teaching can be effective. "First," say Ericsson & Charness (1997), "teachers directly instruct students about some of the knowledge and rules, but....The main core of the acquisition process is based on deliberate practice where future expert performers engage in representative tasks that provide immediate feedback and opportunities for error correction and/or gradual refinement" (p.24). Note the critical importance of the sequence: assessment, feedback, and corrective feedback. This three-step process helps learners both to maintain the level of performance already attained and to improve further (Ericsson & Lehmann, 1996). For a person to become a scholar requires learners to practice their cognitive skills continually far beyond graduation; and to sustain this practice over a lifetime of continuing learning.

A KEY OBSTACLE TO EARLY LEARNING TO LEARN

As hinted at the beginning of this chapter, when teachers strive to help students master early the goal of learning-to-learn, the teachers will find that they have to balance this goal with competing demands for time to master the current subject matter of a discipline or profession. Oftentimes teachers feel that they absolutely "must cover the content." Often this drive is reinforced by a looming deadline for students to pass a licensing examination that consists entirely of questions about current knowledge in the field. What can be done to cope with this obstacle?

A first sensible step is to share the problem with the students. They are unlikely themselves to want to sacrifice content mastery to the effort to become more proficient learners. Ideally, the course syllabus will forewarn of this problem and suggest ways to deal with it. Even if the teacher has some success in "selling" learning-to-learn as a learning goal, students will need help in how to work on it and still reach a timely mastery of the subject matter they seek. Among the ways teachers can help students learn how to learn are arrangements for out-of-class collaborative learning, for out-of-class exercises in checking on knowledge acquired from readings, and for written work complementing in-class instruction (Blaye, Light, Joiner, & Sheldon, 1991).

Concluding Note

No more useful service can be rendered to students than that of enabling them to become effective, self-managing, and self-regulating learners. Doing so requires eliciting students' own deep interests in and commitment to learning. It also requires helping them develop the capacity to plan, evaluate, and manage their learning. A college or university that seeks to become a learning-centered institution will need to transform itself into a learning-centered culture that supports faculty efforts to foster the habits and skills of self-managed learning among its students. Its faculty will need to include a high proportion of practicing expert learners— scholars whose lives are ones of ongoing learning.

REFERENCES

Barr, R. B., & Tagg, J. (1995). From teaching to learning: A new paradigm for undergraduate education. *Change Magazine, 27:* (6) 12-25.

Blaye, A., Light, P., Joiner, R., & Sheldon, S. (1991). Collaboration as a facilitator of planning and problem solving on a computer based task. *British Journal of Developmental Psychology, 94:* (2) 471-483.

Bowne, P. & Engelmann, D. (1999). Improving Effectiveness and Efficiency in Teaching and Learning for Intermediate Students (Alverno College). In M. T. Keeton (Ed.): *Effectiveness and Efficiency in Learning: Case Studies*. Adelphi, MD: Institute for Research on Adults in Higher Education.

Boyatzis, R. E., Cowen, S. S., Kolb, D. A., & Associates. (1995). *Innovation in professional education: Steps on a journey from teaching to learning*. San Francisco: Jossey-Bass.

Broadbent, D. E., FitzGerald, P., & Broadbent, M. H. P. (1986). Implicit and explicit knowledge in the control of complex systems. *British Journal of Psychology, 77*, 33-50.

Brookfield, S. D. (1985). Self-directed learning: A critical review of research. In S. Brookfield (Ed.): *Self-directed learning: From theory to practice*. San Francisco: Jossey-Bass.

Candy, P. (1991). *Self-direction for lifelong learning*. San Francisco: Jossey-Bass.

Cohen, J. (1988). *Statistical power analysis for the behavioral sciences*. Hillsdale, N. J.: Lawrence Erlbaum Associates.

Cohen, J. (1992). A power primer. *Psychological Bulletin, 112:* (1) 155-159.

Ericsson, K. A. & Charness, N. (1994). Expert performance. *American Psychologist, 49*(8), 725-747.

Ericsson, K. A. & Charness, N. (1997). Cognitive and developmental factors in expert performance. In P. J. Feltovich, K. M. Ford, & R. R. Hoffman (Eds.): *Expertise in context: Human and machine*. Cambridge, MA: MIT Press.

Ericsson, K. A. & Lehmann, A. C. (1996). Expert and exceptional performance: Evidence of maximal adaptation to task constraints. *Annual Review of Psychology, 47*, 273-305.

Ertmer, P. G. & Newby, T. J. (1996). The expert learner: Strategic, self-regulated, and reflective. *Instructional Science, 24*, 1-24.

Hellyer, S. (1998, June). Network for excellence in teaching: Faculty helping faculty to facilitate student learning. Paper presented at the Twenty-third UMUC International Conference on Improving University Learning and Teaching, Dublin, Ireland.

Jenkins, R. R. & Romer, K. T. (1998). *Who teaches? Who Learns? Authentic student-faculty partners*. Providence, R.I.: IVY Publishers.

Kluger, A. N. & DeNisi, A. (1996). The effects of feedback interventions on performance: A historical review, a meta-analysis, and a preliminary feedback intervention theory. *Psychological Bulletin, 119:* (2) 254-284.

Knowles, M. (1978). *The adult learner: A neglected species*. (2nd ed.). Houston: Gulf.

Krarabenick, S. & Knapp, J. (1991). Relationship of academic help-seeking to the use of learning strategies and other instrumental achievement behavior in college students. *Journal of Educational Psychology, 83:* (2) 221-230.

Legrow, M., & Sheckley, B. G. (2000). Outcomes of prior vs classroom learning: What are the differences? Paper presented at the International Conference of the Council for Adult and Experiential Learning, Seattle.

Locke, E. A. & Latham, G. P. (1990). Work motivation and satisfaction: Light at the end of the tunnel. *Psychological Science, 1:* (4) 240-246.

McCombs, B. L. & Lauer, P. A. (1998, June). The learner-centered model of seamless professional development: Implications for practice and policy changes in higher education. Paper presented at the Twenty-third UMUC International Conference on Improving University Learning and Teaching, Dublin, Ireland.

Mente, S. (1999). Course Innovations in Developmental Math (Alverno College). In M. T. Keeton (Ed.): *Effectiveness and Efficiency in Learning: Case Studies.* Adelphi, MD: Institute for Research on Adults in Higher Education

Mezirow, J. (1985). A critical theory of self-directed learning. In S. Brookfield (Ed.): *Self-directed learning: From theory to practice.* San Francisco: Jossey-Bass.

Pascarella, E., & Terenzini, P. (1991). *How college affects students: Findings and insights from twenty years of research.* San Francisco: Jossey-Bass.

Reber, A. S. (1993). *Implicit learning and tacit knowledge: An essay on the cognitive unconscious.* New York: Oxford University Press.

Schraw, G. (1998). On the development of adult metacognition. In M. C. Smith & T. Pourchot (Eds.): *Adult learning and development: Perspectives from educational psychology* (pp. 89-106). Mahwah: Lawrence Erlbaum Associates.

Sheckley, B. G. (1984). *Adult learning as a function of temperament, ego-maturity, and perceived locus of control: How individual differences affect adult learning projects.* Unpublished Ph. D. dissertation. University of Connecticut, Storrs.

Solomon, I. (1994). Analogical transfer and "functional fixedness" in the classroom. *Journal of Educational Research, 87:* (6) 371-377.

Sternberg, R. J. (1994). PRSLV: An integrative framework for understanding mind in context. In R. Sternberg & R. Wagner (Eds.): *Mind in context.* Cambridge: Cambridge University Press.

Sternberg, R. J. (1996). *Successful intelligence: How practical and creative intelligence determine success in life.* New York: Plume.

Sternberg, R. J. (1997). Managerial intelligence: Why IQ isn't enough. *Journal of Management, 23:* (3) 475-493.

Tough, A. (1979). *The adult's learning projects: A fresh approach to theory and practice in adult learning.* (2nd ed.). Toronto: Ontario Institute for Studies in Education.

Travers, N. (1998). *Experiential learning and students' self-regulation.* Unpublished doctoral dissertation, University of Connecticut, Storrs.

Travers, N. & Sheckley, B. G. (2000). Changes in students' self-regulation as related to different instructional approaches. Paper presented at the Association for Institutional Research National Forum, Cincinnati.

Voss, J. F. & Post, T. A. (1988). On the solving of ill-structured problems. In M. T. H. Chi, R. Glaser, & M. J. Farr (Eds.): *The Nature of Expertise* (pp. 261-285). Hillsdale: Lawrence Erlbaum Associates.

Wilson, J. M. (1994) The CUPLE physics studio. *The Physics Teacher, 32:* (9) 518-523.

Winne, P. H. (1995a). Inherent details in self-regulated learning. *Educational Psychologist, 30:* (4) 173-187.

Winne, P. H. (1995b). Self-regulation is ubiquitous but its forms vary with knowledge. *Educational Psychologist, 30:* (4) 223-228.

Winne, P. H. (1997). Experimenting to bootstrap self-regulation. *Journal of Educational Psychology, 89:* (3) 397-410.

Witkowski & Magness, D. (1999). Integrated language practice: efficiency and effectiveness in learning (Alverno College). In M.T. Keeton (Ed.): *Effectiveness and Efficiency in Learning: Case Studies.* Adelphi, MD: Institute for Research on Adults in Higher Education.

Zimmerman, B. J. (1990). Self-regulated learning and academic achievement: An overview. *Educational Psychologist, 25:* (1) 3-17.

Zimmerman, B. J. (1994). Dimensions of academic self-regulation: A conceptual framework for education. In D. H. Schunk & B. J. Zimmerman (Eds.): *Self-regulation of learning and performance: Issues and educational applications* (pp. 3-21). Hillsdale: Lawrence Erlbaum Associates.

Zimmerman, B. J. (1995). Attaining reciprocality between learning and development through self-regulation. *Human Development, 38,* 367-372.

Zimmerman, B. J., & Kitsantas, A. (1997). Developmental phases in self-regulation: Shifting from process goals to outcome goals. *Journal of Educational Psychology, 89:*(1) 29-36.

Zimmerman, B. J., & Risemberg, R. (1997). Research for the future: Becoming a self-regulated writer: A social cognitive perspective. *Contemporary Educational Psychology, 22:* (1) 73-101.

Endnote

1. Using the covention for effect size, "d" is the difference between freshmen and seniors expressed in terms of standard deviation (Cohen, 1988). A notation "d = .50" indicates a .50 standard deviation difference between the scores of freshman and seniors. In most cases, d=.30 is interpreted as indicating a "small effect," d=.50, a "medium effect," and d > .80, a "large effect."

CHAPTER 8

Establish a Climate That Enhances Learning

In his research on learning environments during the 1960s George Stern, then at Syracuse University, engaged some 10,000 students in more than 100 colleges and universities, 1000 teachers in 43 public schools, 2500 trainees in 63 Peace Corps programs, and 225 people in five industrial sites. Within each setting Stern found both considerable diversity of individual personalities and also great stability of the overall culture. Overall he found that learning environments included two independent dimensions: (1) self-actualization processes and (2) controls to maintain group structure.

In subsequent studies Stern and colleagues (1970a), using two instruments (the Activities Index and the Environment Index), found that there were five clearly distinguishable types of psychological settings in which American higher education took place, and student personality types were distributed selectively among them.

Institutions of the first type, those with "expressive" cultures, had non-vocational and nonconformist climates. The students in such settings tended to be aesthetic, gregarious, nonpractical, and feminist. At the time of Stern's study Bennington College and Sarah Lawrence, now University, were typical of "expressive" institutions.

The next type, institutions with an "intellectual" culture, were distinguished by an extensive support for intellectual activity, self-expression, and achievement. The students were correspondingly high in intellectual interests and academic motivation. Typical schools were elite liberal arts colleges such as Reed and Swarthmore at the time of the study.

The third type, "protective" institutions, were made up of small denominational colleges that provided a unique cultural setting. This setting consisted of a highly organized supportive environment and a relatively dependent and submissive student body.

Another type of institution, termed "vocational," provided practical instruction for instrumental purposes within a conventionally authoritarian structure.

Students in these institutions tended to be egocentric and self-assertive, as Stern depicted them.

The fifth type, institutions with a "collegiate" culture, were characterized by extensive facilities for student recreation and amusement, close administrative supervision, and relatively low standards of academic achievement. The students were gregarious and self-assertive. The highest collegiate culture scores were associated in the late 1960s with large universities such as the Syracuse and Ohio State of that time.

Stern (1970a) emphasized the cultural stability at each institution. He noted, however, that there was more variation among the students in any of these settings than there was in the environment. Similarly Clark, Trow, Heist and others in the Center for the Study of Higher Education, University of California at Berkeley (1972) found that Stern's cultural types did not exist in pure form at any one college they studied. Times have changed since 1970, so comparable studies today might find different environmental patterns. Even so, to this day the basic picture continues that institutions embody environmental presses that reflect their distinctive missions, student enrollments, size, and funding. An institution's values define its culture and shape the conduct of members within its community.

Principle 8: A Climate That Enhances Learning

For an institution—whether it is a school, a workplace, a residential community, or a university—to assist learners best in their learning, it must embody a pervasive climate of searching and unfettered inquiry, one that simultaneously challenges learners to develop new perspectives and supports them as they do so.

As illustrated in Table 8-1, a number of strategies can be used to implement this principle. The fact that learning may be best facilitated by a climate of inquiry does not mean that all clients will fare best in, or prefer, such a climate. For example, some students may find that the values of a denominational environment provide benefits that override more robust learning in other areas (Reisberg, 1999).

As we understand the work of Stern and his colleague Robert Pace, who continued these inquiries into climates that enhance learning, the type of learning they addressed was what we call "becoming knowledgeable"—mastering the facts, concepts, and investigative methods of academic studies. The activities of intellectual environments that furthered this learning were exposure to differing opinions, discussion, debate, and other forms of active examination of ideas (as discussed in Principle 5, reflecting on experience). These activities were less strong where intercollegiate sports, parties, and other forms of socialization predominated and were also less strong where accepted religious opinion limited the range of ideas that might be challenged with impunity. The research of Stern (1970a) does not tell us,

Table 8-1. Strategies for Immersing Students in a Climate That Enhances Learning

1. Seed the environment with enthusiastic, knowledgeable educators, mentors, instructors, instructional designers, and managers of learning, who communicate with one another informally as well as formally.

2. Create conditions that attract and retain facilitators of others' learning.

3. Model in the governance and management of the institution the commitment to unfettered inquiry.

4. Combine institutional commitment to a set of key values and goals with a willingness to risk further learning by their being questioned.

5. Adhere to the principles of academic freedom for both faculty and students.

6. See that enthusiasm for, and preoccupation with, career and family or community issues, or with athletic and recreational interests do not so contaminate institutional life as to weaken the practiced commitment to learning.

7. Cultivate a cadre of key "influencers" with institutional loyalty who are active "keepers of the ethos" of learning and integrity.

8. Distinguish between being a good instructor/mentor/coach and being an astute co-designer of the institution's philosophy and strategy for learning, and encourage faculty to become expert in both roles.

9. Build into the institution's quality assurance system a periodic evaluation of its performance on Strategies 8-1.1 to 8-1.8.

10. In admissions and retention policies and practices, aim for a productive match between institutional goals and supports on the one hand and individual student aspirations and capabilities on the other hand.

11. Provide a faculty development program that emphasizes efforts to enhance the achieved student learning outcomes, and require periodic participation by instructors.

however, whether *proficiency* as herein defined was better advanced within the environments described.

The research on institutional culture does indicate that the efforts of individual teachers can be substantially enhanced by an institution-wide press for—or diminished by restrictions against—unfettered inquiry in all domains. For maximum effectiveness and efficiency in learning an institution must have a climate or culture of intellectual exploration and questioning.

Research on institutional environments has had especially strong ongoing expression in work using the College Student Experiences Questionnaire (CSEQ), available from the Indiana University Center for Postsecondary Research and Planning. The questionnaire focuses on how students spend their time. It yields a much more complex analysis of the environments than did the studies of thirty years ago, and data are available to facilitate comparison with typical institutions of different sizes, age mixes, ethnic diversity, and sponsorship. The principle bearing on the power of distinctive climates in affecting learning is more readily seen in some of the earlier studies.

COLLEGES WITH DISTINCTIVE CULTURES

In a study of the future of liberal arts colleges that was done in the mid-1960s, some thirty deans and faculty members found that a climate of intellectual inquiry was the one distinguishing characteristic of the best of the colleges (Keeton & Hilberry, 1969). Leaders of these institutions typically held one or more high priority commitments that from time to time evoked challenges from other stakeholders, thus generating a yeasty condition for testing the devotion to inquiry (Strategy 8-1.4).

In most cases commitments that conflicted with a dedication to inquiry were the source of the yeastiness. For example, Earlham College with its Quaker tradition of commitment to consensus in decision-making was so committed to free inquiry that it was often torn by student or faculty pressures to question the practicality and utility of governance by consensus. Wheaton College of Illinois, though requiring faculty members to sign an oath of belief in certain conservative Christian doctrines, encouraged inquiry to a degree that found students questioning these very same doctrines.

The dominant climate of an institution can be formed by different parties. In his book *The Distinctive College* (1970), Burton Clark identified a cadre of influential senior faculty members who filled a role as "preservers of institutional character" in such institutions as Swarthmore College, Reed College, and Antioch College of the mid-20th century. In each of these institutions the originator of the vision and climate of the institution was a charismatic leader such as Swarthmore's Frank Aydelotte or Antioch's Arthur Morgan, and each was followed by one or more presidents or by a corps of influential faculty who helped sustain the culture. When a later generation of "preservers" took on a different array of values (e.g., young Turks at Antioch in the late 1960s who were devotees of their disciplines and unfamiliar with the power of alternative work and study to elicit maturation and proficiency), the earlier character was altered somewhat or even put in jeopardy.

The predominant press or influence of a college community upon its students can also be affected by the makeup of the student body itself. The Office of Institutional Research of Antioch, with the help of a Berkeley study of 1959-1966 found that as Antioch's selectivity grew, as measured by SAT scores, the level of impulsivity of its students also rose, as measured on a scale of the Omnibus Personality Inventory. As selectivity increased, drop-outs among those bright, impulsive students also increased. A task group named by the Dean of Faculty surmised that giving students more choice of what to study and less threat of reduced grades might counteract the impulse to leave. The surmise proved correct as an option for high-SAT students to choose an ungraded first year of studies reversed the drop in persistence rates.

When in the late 1960s and early 1970s Antioch ventured to set up centers for adult learners away from its home campus, it was not feasible to alternate periods of full time study with periods of full time work: most of the adult students had to keep working full time. The climate of inquiry and the strategy of active reflection upon the work were nevertheless preserved in what was called concurrent work and study. In this process, students worked full or part-time in a profession such as counseling, teaching, or government service while using this work experience as a basis for inquiry and reflection during evening or weekend classes on the campus.

Morehouse College of the 1960s saw itself as an instrument of liberation for African-American students. At that time the college respectfully called for the advancement of "Negro" people and viewed education as the most powerful vehicle in that cause. As Elizabeth Geen of Goucher College and Conrad Hilberry of Kalamazoo College wrote:

> Every member of the Morehouse community, regardless of his age, has a stake in unlocking the shackles of the American Negro. The students want to be in white America but not necessarily of it. They want to be able to enjoy Bach without being ashamed of "chittlin culture" (Geen, E. & Hilberry, C., 1969, p. 368).

This combination of faith in learning and a commitment to a burning cause led to Morehouse's graduating distinguished alumni such as Martin Luther King, Jr., who embodied a quality of leadership "that will be constructive and far-seeing" (p. 369). The college did so with limited means and less selectivity than an Amherst College or an Earlham College. Recognizing the institution's distinction in no way denies what Geen and Hilberry (1969) described as also present at the time in "its moments of boastfulness, its perhaps undue emphasis on the Protestant ethic of success, its aping of the white world's fraternities and football queens" (p. 369). The powerful commitment displayed at Morehouse for the greater freedom of African-American students as well as a dominant drive for justice defined its institutional culture. In the 1960s the opportunities for African-American leadership were primarily in the religious ministry and teaching, but students at Morehouse College were preparing to take positions at IBM, at General Motors, in the federal judiciary, in states senates, or among the scholars and presidents of colleges. A change in campus culture was also in the making.

Amherst College. Amherst students of the mid-1960s, according to Stevens of Reed College and Alexander of Antioch College (Keeton, 1969), were bright, assertive, and "had it all."

> In any description of Amherst, 'affluence' must be a key word, encompassing not only endowment and gifts but the varied riches that often accompany these—prestige, faculty with national reputations, students

with high aptitude scores, excellent records in school, and well-educated parents, a low student-faculty ratio, relatively light teaching loads, and excellent buildings and facilities (Stevens & Alexander, 1969, p. 150).

A sharper contrast than that with Morehouse of the same period would be hard to find; but both colleges were highly productive of capable graduates, and both combined a culture of play with one of inquiry. Amherst was engaged at the time as well in a serious re-examination of its own educational program—another form of serious inquiry.

Establishing an Institutional Culture That Enhances Learning

Unfortunately studies of institutional climate since the 1970s no longer focus as clearly as did these studies on the press for inquiry. There are, however, numerous universities and colleges with a primary mission of teaching which have developed a variety of ways of furthering this mission in ways adapted to their differing clienteles. It is clear also that no one culture serves all students. Different students thrive best in different climates. If institutional leaders discern a mismatch in values among their stakeholders or between shared commitments and the resources for implementing them, a strategy for correcting the mismatch is needed. (Strategy 8-1.9). That strategy will need to derive from an analysis of the causes of the mismatch. A public university governed by trustees hostile to academic freedom presents a much more formidable problem for correction than does the lack of know-how by the academic management as to how to conduct faculty development for teaching online. A private college short of resources for distance education and seeking to serve a distant adult population faces a choice of either mustering the resources or giving up on the new niche to which it aspires. There are, in any case, significant ways in which the climate that enhances learning can be enhanced by a focus on supporting the learning efforts of staff and students.

Institutions that are acclaimed for enhancing student learning in environments of unfettered inquiry have a number of distinctive features. The people in charge are preoccupied with enhancing student learning. The institution exhibits a climate of mutual respect and of collaboration in a significant cause. A sense of being and belonging in a learning community permeates the institution. The institution "practices what it preaches" by focusing on optimizing achievement through inquiry rather than maintaining safer, unquestioned practices. Above all, the institution has a determination among all its stakeholders to further knowledge, understanding, and proficiency among its graduates.

Rare is the college or university that does not want to be more supportive of teachers' efforts to facilitate students' learning and of students' efforts to learn more effectively. Administrators, however, are often confronted with crises or what seem to be more pressing problems; and among teachers there is often a lack of a clear set of strategies and tactics to achieve the result they seek. From the case studies and recent research we have studied, a number of promising strategies and tactics emerge.

In times past the norm among most academic administrations was to provide faculty with office space, classrooms, and library and then to leave faculty to their own devices—an arrangement cherished by faculty as contrasted with an atmosphere restrictive of academic freedom. Such supports are by no means adequate to the conditions under which faculty now function at the beginning of the twenty-first century. Today a university such as UMUC offers an annual opportunity for faculty to compete for research awards intended to know more about improving instruction, especially for online students. Many institutions have created Centers for Teaching Excellence to encourage faculty efforts to improve instruction. As outlined in Table 8-2, a number of ways are available that can enhance the effectiveness of instructors and support staff in their efforts to enhance learning.

Adopt continuing steps that support teachers' efforts to enhance learning. Teachers benefit from support that enables them to devote time to the improvement of their teaching. Such assistance helps teachers to identify practices that could be improved and resources to help them to refine past practices. McKeachie (1994) recommends that teachers use a variety of sources in learning how to improve: "student ratings, peer visitations, group interviews, peer evaluation of syllabi, examinations and student products, and development of a portfolio of various kinds of data" (p. 314). In a study at the University of Michigan, teachers reported that the most helpful process included combining use of such evidence with consultation that provided encouragement and suggested alternative teaching strategies (p. 321)."

At Alverno College faculty meet together in plenary sessions, committees, or task groups every Friday afternoon during instruction periods to discuss curriculum

---

Table 8-2. Strategies for Supporting Teachers

1. Adopt continuing steps that support teachers' efforts to enhance learning.

2. Give frequent help in teachers' evaluating their own teaching and in consultation on how to improve.

3. Provide faculty with efficient ways of tapping the best of current intellectual resources.

4. Provide time and respect for good teaching.

5. Provide teaching assistance in ways that enhance learning by the students rather than saving teacher time at the expense of student learning.

6. Support the training of teaching assistants as well as that of full-time and adjunct faculty.

---

and instruction matters. In addition, Alverno faculty members engage in continuous and longitudinal research on the teaching effectiveness of the institution and of its specific curricular and instructional efforts. Task groups of Alverno faculty devise innovations in teaching and follow through with evaluation and feedback to further improvement. Public recognition of good performance is also a normal part of the College's life.

Few colleges can arrange scheduling of faculty time as Alverno does, but most colleges could arrange for substantially more collaborative faculty work on educational strategy, instructional planning, innovative projects in teaching, and workshops for teaching improvement. Normally the use of time in these ways needs to be offset by reduction of other less productive uses of the instructors' time.

The University of South Australia (UofSA) has adopted a strategy that, like Alverno's, defines clearly the qualities a graduate should embody, but deploys faculty and staff effort differently to reach the goal. UofSA advocates what it calls a "student-centered and process-driven methodology" of learning. This strategy mandates that all instruction should be focused on developing graduates who:

- operate effectively with and upon a body of knowledge in sufficient depth to begin professional practice;
- are prepared for lifelong learning in pursuit of personal development and excellence in professional practice;
- are effective problem solvers, capable of applying logical, critical, and creative thinking to a range of problems;
- can work autonomously and collaboratively as professionals;
- are committed to ethical action and social responsibility as professionals and as citizens;
- communicate effectively in professional practice and as members of communities; and
- demonstrate an international perspective as professionals and citizens.

To assure that these qualities are fostered by instruction the University employs an array of procedures to develop understanding of the qualities, commitment to their development, and ownership of the responsibility for achieving them (Feast & Barrett, 1999). These procedures include establishing a well-developed, explicit framework of values (in this case the "graduate qualities" being sought), using course development teams that work collaboratively; building an atmosphere of trust and collegiality; providing recognition by institutional leaders for the expertise of the implementing staff; and providing resources adequate to the tasks.

Give frequent help to teachers in evaluating their teaching. Normal practice provides teachers with little time for evaluating and re-planning their practices and for developing more sophisticated instructional tactics. The evaluation of faculty performance may be done once a year or less often by way of a staff assistant's distributing forms for gathering students' assessments of teaching. In an ideal situation, students give interpretive comments on their ratings. In addition, a supervisor (department chair or dean) or a fellow faculty member could review and reflect with the teacher upon the student comments.

Teachers who take charge of the evaluation and re-shaping of their own teaching are often conflicted as to how much time to take away from classroom instruction or from students' out-of-class study time to solicit their opinions and insights. They wrestle with how best to use this time. Angelo and Cross (1993) address these questions most helpfully, as do also Rando and Lenze (1994 NCTLA). For example, Angelo and Cross (1993) suggest that faculty build ongoing formative evaluations into their courses. One technique they suggest is for faculty to ask students, at the end of a class session, to write down on an index card two or three sentences on what they learned during the class, what questions remain as they exit the class, or what issues they would like to follow up on in the next session. This exercise requires only two or three minutes of class time, but provides rich information that can help instructors improve their effectiveness. In general, time devoted to helping teachers evaluate and improve their instructional skills can pay off handsomely as compared with alternative uses of the same time.

Provide faculty with efficient ways of tapping the best of current intellectual resources. Educators are used to emphasizing the teachers' need for ample libraries, laboratories, studios, support staff, and the working tools of the trade. As we have discussed earlier, with some institutional strategies such as cooperative education, an entire array of staff and cooperative arrangements with other organizations may be involved in "equipping the teachers."

Today teachers need access to tools such as computers, institutionally maintained communication systems, the Internet, or even such technologies as compressed video, videocassettes, and the like (Skinner, 1998). Sometimes the purchase of a book or a subscription to a journal can provide teachers with resources to improve their craft. Under the pressure of legislators and tuition-payers to cut the costs of education, teachers and their administrators will now have to struggle with the choice as to which resources and tools are essential, affordable, and usable in cost effective ways.

In this day of the Internet and related telecommunications tools, the intellectual resources to which faculty and students have access are enormously greater than even a quarter century ago. But access to "garbage" has escalated by at least as high an order of magnitude. Today's student can sit in the university's computer lab or at home and examine the contents of great libraries anywhere in the world and can have abstracts of articles or the full text printed out on the spot. In this circumstance faculty members need to know not only their own specialties, but also who knows best about related disciplines and how to find the best intellectual resources. Intellectual expertise becomes a matter of how best to evaluate and use intellectual resources. At a quite recent time a college student had only the use of textbooks, the college's own library and faculty, and sometimes a cumbersome interlibrary loan service. Those were the limits of resources available. Today learners can easily be overwhelmed with unmanageably rich resources. An early task of becoming a competent, effectively functioning lifelong learner is to master the skills of best use of the ever-growing and ever more complex treasury of intellectual resources.

When reformers such as the authors urge faculty to lecture less or not at all, the faculty may feel that there is no respect left for expert knowledge or for teachers who see their primary role as that of researcher in a discipline or profession. We take an opposite view. We believe that teachers should be masters of the content of the fields in which they teach and, when they function as assessors, they should likewise do so as experts in what they are assessing.

Given this point of view, how can teachers elicit learning by students in the most efficient way? The issue is not whether expertise among teachers is needed, but how best to make use of their expertise. The tension is between conveying teachers' knowledge to students while also helping students to develop expertise themselves.

For most instructors good teaching takes extraordinary time and effort. Minimizing the use of lectures and using them for only what they can do best, as we suggest, requires greater skill, more time, and deeper understanding of the subject than does most lecturing. "Telling students the answers" elicits little learning because genuine learning requires the learner to construct ideas that explain a growing body of experience or do so in ways that improve the ability to foresee consequences and solve problems. Hence, time and respect for that evocative work are necessary.

If teaching is poorly rewarded or not at all, instructors will have little incentive to strive for efficiency in teaching since the level of effort required will demand dedication, continuous attention to evaluation, and concentrated efforts to improve. Given reasonable pay, the rewards most motivating for teachers tend to be those of respect (including self-respect), admiration of colleagues and students, and support for the work of improvement (Schunk, 1990; Silver, Mitchell et al., 1995; Tannenbaum, 1997). If teachers' duties are so defined as to preclude the needed level of effort for providing excellent instruction (e.g., excessive administrative tasks, a priority focus on research, or emphasis on non-teaching service activities), teachers are less likely to perform in a superior way.

In today's universities with a high proportion of adult students and adjunct faculty, administrators can cultivate specialization within a cadre of faculty, with a small proportion of full-time academic managers who then relieve the part-time teachers of all duties except teaching (Harvey & Knight 1996; Bell, Hugetz et al. 1998). In this scenario, part-time instructors would ideally complement their teaching with practice and research in the specialization with their other employers. In addition, a faculty development program and evaluation procedures that press for searching inquiry can help faculty develop skills for working effectively with adult learners who are concerned with advancing in their own careers.

Provide teaching assistance in ways that enhance learning by the students rather than saving teacher time at the expense of student learning. The damaging practice of using graduate students untutored in good teaching practice to save faculty time needs no elaboration here. Faculty can, however, deploy assistants (graduate and undergraduate) in ways that foster the learning of all involved. The Wisconsin Emerging Scholars Program (Chapter 4, pages 35 and 36) and its predecessor forms of similar practice provide one model. The engagement of upperclass undergraduates in faculty research in the students' areas of concentration is another readily adaptable model of good practice.

Shift the metaphor for learning and instruction. This chapter focuses on establishing a climate of learning. If, however, learning is thought of as simply memorizing and repeating information provided by others, the results of which we write will not occur. If learning to learn is a matter of functioning like computers, the task of facilitating learning is less beneficial and less challenging than we urge. To transform students' understanding of human experience, the concept of learning and instruction must involve a shift from that of merely accumulating knowledge and retrieving it to one of participating in its further development and transformation.

Oftentimes the practices used by teachers who advocate "telling students the answers" are grounded in a long-standing metaphor of how students learn. Since the 1940s the metaphors of "mind-as-computer" and "learning-as-information-processing" have dominated educational practices (Mayer, 1996). The basis for the metaphor is the input-throughput-output design of a computer. This design has four key components. First, the system requires specific hardware (monitor, memory capacity, processor, printer, etc.) to perform the input-throughput-output tasks. Second, the data to be analyzed must be accessible to the computer usually in the form of a file stored on a disk or hard drive. Third, if the task involves analyzing a specific data file, the software to conduct the analysis must be present. Finally, for its most effective operation, the computer and its components should be located in a temperature-controlled room with electrical outlets, lights, computer resources (e.g., disks, paper for printers), and connections that allow networking with other computers.

Learning processes, when depicted as "computer-like," are described as occurring serially, one after another. The senses (keyboard) activate a step by step process in which the cerebral cortex (computer processor) pulls information from memory (the hard drive files). Then a cognitive activity such as reasoning (software program) is used to analyze the information. Frequently the output of one cognitive process (e.g., a discrete piece of information) becomes the input for a second cognitive process. These processes continue in serial order as the output of the second cognitive process (again a discrete piece of information) becomes the input for a third process, and so on.

Instruction, following this model, involves teachers dispensing information through lectures so that learners can encode this information into memory structures in a way that would enable these learners to retrieve the information in a future situation (e.g., question on a final exam or problem in a work setting). Knowledge, in this model is reflected in (a) the amount and types of information stored in memory, (b) the ability to recall this stored information, and (c) the ability to use this information in a variety of situations (e.g., problem solving situations) (Mayer, 1992).

Researchers such as LeDoux (1996) who explore how the mind works go to great lengths to point out that their work does not fall prey to the "despised computer metaphor." For example, Damasio (1994), Edelman (1991), Sylwester (1995), and other critics of the mind-as-computer metaphor spotlight the following flaws in the mind-as-computer analogy.

- Computers operate in series, doing one thing at a time; brains operate in parallel, carrying out millions of actions at the same time.
- Computers have a limited number of connections; brains have trillions—and can create more.
- Computers are designed to operate based on laws of physics and mechanics; brains operate as biological organs influenced by genes, hormones, and chemicals.
- Computers are standardized according to a set of manufacturing specifications; brains are unique, they assemble themselves based on an individual's experiences, environmental influences, and genetic codes.
- The meaning of symbols entered into a computer is predetermined, assigned by a human programmer; the meaning of symbols entering the mind from the senses is indeterminate; meaning is constructed from a history of present and past interactions with the world.
- Computers accurately and effectively process complex sequences of clearly defined facts; brains conceptualize ambiguous problems by identifying definitive and value-laden elements that they can incorporate into an acceptable solution.

Many researchers question outright the adequacy of the learning-as-information processing metaphor. For example, Alba and Hasher (1983) state that a considerable body of research findings exists that is not easily accounted for by the major assumptions of the information-processing model. "Our review of the literature suggests that memory for complex events is far more detailed than schematic processes would allow" (p. 225).

In his critique of the mind-as-computer metaphor, Edelman (1991) notes that the metaphor of mind-as-computer is a fallacy of logic known as "category error." A person who commits this error would not recognize the different meanings of the words "golf" and "clubs" in the following phrase: Members of golf clubs use clubs to golf. Individuals who commit category errors are prone to fallacies of reasoning such as interpreting readings of instruments on an airplane panel as if they were readings from instruments on the dashboard of a car—or likening the processing of information in a computer to processing of information by a brain. For this reason as well as those listed above, Edelman (1991) characterizes the analogy as an "embarrassment." He argues that "little or nothing of value can be gained from the application of this failed analogy between the computer and the brain" (p. 227).

In addition to providing a flawed basis for development of theory, the mind-as-computer metaphor has a final and very serious limitation. As a guide for instruction, it is not effective. Numerous research studies (Baldwin & Ford, 1988; Tannenbaum, 1997) indicate that only about 10% to 20% of information learned in formats that follow the mind-as-computer model is ever used outside of classroom settings.

Make Learning Feasible and Rewarding for Students

We should do for students just what we have been talking of doing for teachers: make the learning activities feasible and rewarding for them. Table 8-3 lists illustrative practices that can accomplish this goal.

STUDY AND ADAPT FOR DIFFERENT PROFILES OF RISK AND PROMISE

Some students learn no matter how poor or good the teaching, and some students frustrate the best of teacher efforts. But normally effective learning results from the interplay of good practice on the part of both teachers and students. As reported in Chapter 4, the 1992-1997 studies by the IRAHE Diverse Students Program (DSP) searched for patterns of student characteristics and institutional features that were most predictive of high risk of dropping out and of high promise of successful performance by students (Cubeta, Travers et al., 2001). The patterns thus disclosed were used by UMUC and Prince George's Community College (MD), with quite different student bodies, to define "profiles" of high risk and high promise. Prince George's went on to devise, as described earlier, the very successful 3-Cubed Academy for two of its ten high risk profiles of students. Strategies and tactics for use of this knowledge are illustrated in Chapter 4, Table 4-1.

Table 8-3. Strategies for Making Learning Rewarding for Students

---

1. Study and adapt for different profiles of risk and promise among students.

2. Provide opportunities for students to use first-hand experience to test theories and deepen their understanding of them and of the field of study (Ch. 5).

3. Where external obstacles face students on matters with which the university or college cannot be of direct help, provide counsel and contacts through which the obstacles can be overcome.

4. Emphasize with faculty and staff the respecting of all students and helping all personnel to combine realism about students' prospects for learning with that respect.

Since no two students have the same interests, talents, or circumstances, and since teachers rarely know all of these things at the outset of instruction, the task of appropriately encouraging and supporting students can be quite challenging, sending academic administrators back to the feasibility of the task for instructors! Indeed, most colleges and universities tend to regard as impractical thorough, ongoing individualization of instruction. We believe, on the contrary, that if effective learning is the goal, the drive toward maximum feasible individualization must be pursued in ways that do not cater to students' weaknesses, but optimize their strengths. Ways to do so have by now been described and illustrated in this book. To recapitulate, they include:

- finding links between the learning goals of instruction and vital interests of the students, thus adding to their motivation to learn (Principle 6);
- establishing goals early and reviewing, clarifying, and revising them as needed (Principle 1);
- helping students become more effective learners, including ways to use their time more efficiently (Principle 7);
- relative to student capability, setting high expectations and providing matching supports (Principle 3);
- doing an early diagnosis of students' intellectual functioning, interests, values, and habits relative to their learning plans, and enabling them to get appropriate help in remedying or strengthening areas in which so doing will save effort (Principle 3);
- within courses or other learning processes, giving frequent assessment of progress and helpful feedback on learning from mistakes and planning next steps (Principle 2);
- avoiding the waste of students' time on needless or relatively useless tasks or through inconvenient scheduling and siting of instruction;
- providing other supports for using time effectively, such as via the new technologies and by providing repeated opportunity to apply concepts and information in diverse contexts (Principle 5);
- using first-hand experience to test theories and deepen understanding of them and of the field of study (Principle 4);
- helping students learn to become more proficient in learning collaboratively (Principle 5);
- enabling students to use the new technologies more effectively;
- treating students respectfully and supporting their self-esteem and realism about their own potential and prospects (Principle 3); and
- assisting students in finding outside support to cope with external obstacles to their success in college (Principle 3).

The sections that follow outline further ways to support student effort. These strategies are essential strategies for fostering a pervasive climate of learning.

Provide opportunities for students to use first-hand experience to test theories and deepen their understanding of their use within a field of study (Principle 4).

Older adult students tend to be quick to test theories propounded in class with what they have learned at work or in civic service or leisure pursuits (Kolb, 1984). Orchestrating an ideal interplay of personal experience with theoretical study is more difficult with 18- to 22-year-olds. For young students the predominance of information processing in instruction is particularly problematic because of the limited scope and variety of their experience base (Principle 4). For more experienced adults instructors must avoid walling off students' work life from their activities as students. Instead, instructors can learn enough of students' work lives to encourage cross-reflection by the students toward the goal of helping students integrate their work experience with current topics they are studying.

Teach students to help each other learn; that is, build habits of collaboration and options for collaboration on course assignments and projects in ways integral to the goals of study (Principle 5). Reference has been made to this strategy in Chapter 5. The literature on ways students can learn collaboratively is enormous (Blaye, Light, et. al., 1991; Brookfield, 1986; Markus, Howard, & King, 1993). The study of supplemental instruction at University of Missouri-Kansas City (Wilcox, 1999) shows a documented application of this idea to "high-risk courses." The case study from the University of Connecticut (Kehrhahn, Sheckley, Travers, 2000) shows how learners working together collaboratively on research teams enriched their doctoral studies. A wide variety of other applications is described in the literature (Blaye, Light et al. 1991). In cases where collaboration is most effective, it is concentrated in higher order thinking tasks, such as critique of ideas, construction of alternative interpretations of data, and application of concepts to diverse problems. It is not used to help students simply grasp basic concepts or memorize facts.

Where external obstacles face students on matters with which the university or college cannot be of direct help, provide counsel and contacts through which the obstacles can be overcome (Principle 4). The School for New Resources of the College of New Rochelle has done outstanding work in facilitating problem-solving for students of color who come with multiple obstacles to college learning. These obstacles include: low household income, unfamiliarity with bureaucratic practices essential to their gaining support, poor schooling, family background lacking anyone with previous college experience, and lack of support at home or in the worksite for coping with these difficulties. To help students overcome these many impediments the College offers an array of services such as childcare, transportation, financial loans for both college and personal expenses, tutorial services, peer counseling, frequent skill assessments, remediation, easy access to instructors, and assistance finding jobs.

Emphasize with faculty and staff the respecting of all students and helping all personnel to combine realism about students' prospects for learning with that respect. Many students are handicapped by fearfulness and underestimation of their potential for learning or their sense of not being accepted as legitimate members of the academic community (Cubeta, Travers et al., 2001). While overconfidence and false pride can be damaging to effective learning, a more frequent barrier to academic success is self-doubt or non-acceptance by peers and institutional staff (Baldwin, Carrell et al., 1990; Anderson, Glassman et al., 1995). Extensive work has gone into documenting the damage to women learners by the misconception that they lack ability in mathematical studies (Belenky, McVicker Clinchy et al., 1986). Where the seeds of doubt have been firmly planted, teachers and support staff will need to work on their removal early in the course of instruction at college level.

Where students come into college with weak educational background from school and family conditions, they need to be assisted in seeing how this initial handicap can be overcome and in understanding that the handicap is not an irremovable one (Phipps, 1998).

A Concluding Note

There is no more fundamental foundation for an institution's efficiency in furthering student learning than the priorities among the values that shape its climate and the extent to which that climate presses its students toward a lifetime of continuing inquiry. Given that commitment, the ways of implementing it are legion. Significant among such ways are strategies that give support to faculty and student efforts to carry out well their respective roles in furthering intellectual inquiry.

REFERENCES

Alba, J. W. & L. Hasher (1983). Is memory schematic? *Psychological Bulletin 93:* (2) 203-231.

Anderson, S. M., & N. S. Glassman, et al. (1995). Transference in social perception: The role of chronic accessibility in significant-other representations. *Journal of Personality and Social Psychology 69:* (1) 41-57.

Angelo, T. A. & Cross, K. P. (1993). *Classroom assessment techniques: A handbook for college teachers. 2nd Edition.* San Francisco: Jossey-Bass.

Baldwin, M. W., Carrell, S. E., et al. (1990). Priming relationship schemas: My advisor and the pope are watching me from the back of my mind. *Journal of Experimental Social Psychology 26:* 435-454.

Baldwin, T. T. & J. K. Ford (1988). Transfer of training: A review and directions for future research. *Personnel Psychology:* 63-105.

Belenky, M. F., McVicker Clinchy, N., et al. (1986). *Women's ways of knowing: The development of self, voice, and mind.* New York, NY, Basic Books, Inc.

Bell, D., Hugetz, E., et al. (1998). *Toward a pluralistic future: Institutional reform and the multiversity.* Improving University Learning and Teaching, Dublin.

Blaye, A., Light, P., Joiner, R., & King, D. C. (1991). Collaboration as a facilitator of planning and problem solving on a computer based task. *British Journal of Developmental Psychology 9*: 471-483.

Brookfield, S. D. (1986). *Understanding and facilitating adult learning.* San Francisco: Jossey-Bass.

Clark, B. R. (1970). *The distinctive college: Swarthmore, Reed, Antioch.* Chicago: Aldine Publishing Company.

Clark, B. R., Trow, M., Heist, P., & Associates (1972). *Students and colleges: Interaction and change.* Berkeley: University of California Center for Research and Development in Higher Education.

Coleman, J. (1976). Differences between experiential and classroom learning. In M. T. Keeton and Associates: *Experiential learning: Rationale, characteristics, and assessment.* San Francisco: Jossey-Bass Publishers.

Cubeta, J., Travers, N., et al. (2001). Predicting academic success of adults from diverse populations. *Journal of College Student Retention: Research, Theory, & Practice 2:* (4) 297-313.

Cubeta, J., Travers, N., & Sheckley, B. G. (1998). Predicting the academic success of adults from diverse populations, in *Journal of Higher Education* [in press].

Damasio, A. R. (1994). *Descartes' error: Emotion, reason, and the human brain.* New York, NY, Avon Books.

Edelman, G. M. (1991). *Bright air, brilliant fire: On the matter of the mind.* New York, BasicBooks.

Feast, V. & Barrett, S. (1999). Mainstreaming graduate qualities in a business and management faculty core: An exercise in educational contracting. Paper presented at the International Conference on Improving University Learning and Teaching, Brisbane, Australia.

Geen, E. & Hilberry, C. (1969). Morehouse College. In M. T. Keeton & C. Hilberry: *Struggle and promise: A future for colleges.* New York: McGraw-Hill Book Company.

Harvey, L. & Knight, P. T. (1996). *Transforming higher education.* Buckingham, UK, The Society for Research into Higher Education & The Open University Press.

Keeton, M. T. & Hilberry, C., (Eds.). (1969). *Struggle and promise: A future for colleges.* New York: McGraw Hill Book Co.

Keeton, M. T., Clagett, C. A., & Engleberg, I. N. (1998). Improving minority student success: Crossing boundaries and making connections between theory, research, and academic planning. Workshop at the 1998 International Conference of the Society for College and University Planning, Vancouver, B.C., Canada. IRAHE Research Papers. College Park, MD: IRAHE/UMUC.

Kehrhahn, M., Sheckley, B. G., & Travers, N. L. (2000). *Efficiency and effectiveness in graduate education: A case analysis.* (Vol. 76): Association for Institutional Research.

Kolb, D. A. (1984). *Experiential learning: Experiences as the source of learning and development.* Englewood Cliffs, Prentice-Hall.

LeDoux, J. (1996). *The emotional brain: The mysterious underpinnings of emotional life.* New York, Simon & Schuster.

Lewin, K. (1947). Frontiers in group dynamics: Concept, method, and reality in social science. *Human Relations, 1,* 5-41.

Markus, G. B., Howard, J. P. F., & King, D. C. (1993). Integrating community service and classroom instruction enhances learning: Results from an experiment. *Educational Evaluation & Policy Analysis, v 15,* 410-419.

Mayer, R. E. (1992). Cognition and instruction: Their historic meeting within educational psychology. *Journal of Educational Psychology 84:* (4) 405-412.

Mayer, R. E. (1996). Learners as information processors: Legacies and limitations of educational psychology's second metaphor. *Educational Psychologist 31:* (3/4) 151-161.

Phipps, R. (1998). College remediation: What it is, what it costs, what's at stake. Washington D.C., The Institute for Higher Education Policy: 1-26.

Rando, W. C. & Lenz, L. F. (1994). *Learning from students: Early-term student feedback in higher eduation.* State College, Pennsylvania: NCTLA.

Reisberg, L. (1999, March 5). Enrollments surge in Christian colleges. *In The Chronicle of Higher Education,* A42.

Schunk, D. H. (1990). Goal setting and self-efficacy during self-regulated learning. *Educational Psychologist 25:* (1) 71-86.

Silver, W. S., Mitchell, T. R., et al. (1995). Responses to successful and unsuccessful performance: The moderating effect of self-efficacy on the relationship between performance and attributions. *Organizational Behavior and Human Decision Processes 62:* (3) 286-299.

Skinner, R. A. (1998). Moving from the information age to the age of learning: What happens when everyone in a college is "connected"? Improving University Learning and Teaching, Dublin.

Stern, G. (1970a). *People in Context.* New York: John Wiley & Sons.

Stern, G. (1970b). People in Context, Presentation at a symposium on "Human Behavior and Its Control," American Association for the Advancement of Science, December 30, 1970. Chicago, IL.

Stevens, C. M. & Alexander, W. B. (1969). Amherst College. In M. T. Keeton & C. Hilberry (Eds.): *Struggle and promise: A future for colleges.* New York: McGraw-Hill Book Company.

Sylwester, R. (1995). *A celebration of neurons: An educator's guide to the human brain.* Alexandria, Association for Supervision and Curriculum Development.

Tannenbaum, S. I. (1997). Enhancing continuous learning: Diagnostic findings from multiple companies. *Human Resource Management 36:* (4) 437-452

Wilcox, F. K. (1999). Supplemental instruction in high-risk courses. In M.T. Keeton (Ed.): *Efficiency in adult higher education: Case studies.* Adelphi, MD: Institute for Research on Adults in Higher Education.

Wilson, J. W. & Lyons, E. H. (1961). *Work-study college programs: Appraisal and report of the study of cooperative education.* New York, NY: Harper & Row.

CHAPTER 9

Capitalize on Emerging Technologies

An Early Experience with Distance Education

Just a few years ago (circa 1992-1993) efforts in distance learning were carried out using technologies that were primarily video and print-based. Old Dominion's Teletechnet (1995-1996) was typical of such efforts implemented by a number of institutions at that time to serve nontraditional adult learners. Teletechnet enabled working adults to complete four-year degrees in human services counseling, criminal justice, engineering technology, and nursing. In 1996-97, Teletechnet sites enrolled a total of 5,012 individual students. Of this total approximately 110 were enrolled at sites located within 30 miles of Old Dominion at Norfolk, Virginia, students who presumably could have attended the campus-based program. Program administrators estimated that over 4,000 of the enrollees would not have otherwise participated in public higher education; thus Teletechnet increased 1996 public higher education participation rates in Virginia by about 3.3%. The distance enrollment was projected to double in 1997-98.

Retention in the programs offered through Teletechnet has been very high. Ninety-four percent of the degree-seeking students who enrolled in fall 1994, the first semester of Teletechnet, re-enrolled in the spring of 1995; 92% of those students re-enrolled in courses the following fall semester. Additionally, Teletechnet students were as likely to finish a degree program within two calendar years as were on-campus transfer students. Despite the fact that they worked more hours during the week, 37% of these working adults completed their degree in two years.

Several measures of learning outcomes demonstrated that graduates from the online program demonstrated the same or superior learning gains as compared with students in the conventional face-to-face program. An evaluation of the counseling services program, for example, included ratings provided by both students and internship counselors. The results indicated that there were no differences between students who participated in face-to-face courses and their online counterparts in competency areas such as specific counseling skills, oral and writ-

ten communication skills, listening skills, problem-solving, theoretical knowledge, and awareness of diverse clientele. In other programs, the Teletechnet students showed the same or somewhat better performance in capstone courses (California State University System, 1999, January).

Overview of This Chapter

Throughout this book we have cited instances in which the principles of learning have been applied in distance learning as well as in traditional classrooms. These examples have focused on ways in which the use of emerging technologies has led to efficiencies in instruction. But there are two further ways in which the benefits of the emerging technologies can be enhanced. First, in an area that is usually thought of as administrative they can save institutions the costs of adding new buildings to accommodate larger enrollments, and they can save learners significant costs in commuting time, provisions for child care, and convenience in accommodating other needs of work and family. In addition, more astute managing of use of the technologies in instruction itself and innovations in instruction made possible by uses of the Web can further improve effectiveness and efficiency in learning. In this chapter we give attention to these further aspects of the use of the new technologies. In the chapter that follows we will then seek an overview of other administrative strategies that can be of substantial help in an institution's overall striving for efficiency in learning.

First, however, to summarize the benefits of the emerging technologies in instruction itself, the available educational applications are considerable (Institute for Higher Education Policy, 1999). These applications range from video-conferencing to computer-based instruction and Web-based computer conferencing. Differentiated staffing, structured learning experiences, assessment with corrective feedback, deliberative practice, experience and reflection, communities of learning: all can be fostered quite systematically by the new technologies (Jonassen & Reeves, 1996; Berge, 1997; Haughey & Anderson, 1998; Porter, 1997; Potter, 1998; Roblyer, Edwards & Havriluk, 1997). These methods of mediated instruction or distributed learning (MI/DL[1]) can not only enhance learning but can also reduce costs related to student time and faculty time. Once again, case studies will help us to investigate the unprecedented tools with which we can now create learning environments and assess their costs and benefits.

Perhaps the most easily demonstrated benefit of the new technological applications to education is that of access for populations hitherto unable to continue formal learning (Institute for Higher Education Policy, 1999). For adults to learn most

---

[1] MI/DL is a term adopted to refer to instruction that is delivered substantially by means of electronic/communications technology to sites on or off campus

efficiently, obstacles to access (time, distance, cost) must be removed or minimized. The Old Dominion case is a story that has been told at many other institutions.

The benefits of enhanced learning outcomes, however, have yet to be fully identified (Institute for Higher Education Policy, 1999). Too often we have been satisfied to find "no significant difference" (Russell, 1999) between methods of mediated and distance learning and conventional classrooms. A recent summary of the findings of 15 studies comparing the effectiveness of Asynchronous Learning Networks (ALN) with that of face-to-face classes reported that about 66% of the ALN offerings were more effective, with the remaining comparisons showing no significant differences in learning (Hiltz, 1997; Hiltz & Turoff, 2000).

ACCESS AND RETENTION

A fundamental policy question facing U. S. higher education is how to assure access to postsecondary education for a broad segment of the population in order to insure their participation in the information age workforce. In a time when demographics project an increased enrollment demand beyond what existing college facilities and staff can accommodate, new means of delivery are critical. Historically, print-based correspondence study provided access to learners otherwise constrained by obstacles to further education. Now, mediated instruction and distributed learning (MI/DL) have extended that potential. There is great hope that learning distributed via the newer technologies will answer society's need, and do so at less cost than that of building new campuses or buildings (Massey and Zemsky, 1995; Arvan, 1997; Institute for Higher Education Policy, 1999).

The integration of Asynchronous Learning Network (ALN) technology with Spanish 210 at University of Illinois at Urbana-Champaign demonstrates access of another kind (Arvan, Ory, Bullock, Burnaska & Hanson, 1998). At UIUC, as at many other institutions, the student demand for Spanish far exceeds the department's ability to staff sections. Increased emphasis on internationalism and foreign language requirements has exacerbated this access problem. Initially, two of nine regular sections were taught using ALN; the ALN sections met only once a week (instead of three times per week for conventional classes) and caps on class size were doubled—from 20 to 40 students. The following semester all sections were taught using ALN and all doubled in enrollment. Although students in conventional face-to-face classes outperformed their ALN counterparts on the first mid-term exam, there was no difference in performance on subsequent exams.

In this introductory course, students in the ALN sections had significantly less contact with peers and instructors than did students in the conventional sections. To compensate for the decrease in face-to-face contact instructors increased their availability through expanded office hours. Students, however, apparently were getting the information they needed online. They did not get in touch with the instructors for help. As a result, instructors were able to decrease their office hours. With the staff time thus saved the department has since decided to enrich the course's grammar study with oral conversation skill development. The department is also developing a Web-based version of the Spanish 100-level sequence.

In distance education programs the opportunity costs of narrow access and low retention rates are significant; initial investments in technology must be compared with the "savings" and benefit represented by better access and retention. Historically, correspondence study has had a non-completion rate as high as 50 percent; retention rates with other technologies in which more timely interaction and feedback were possible ranged from 30-50% (Frankola, 2001). As we learn more about effective teaching through the use of technology and as computer conferencing capability has enhanced interactivity, the withdrawal rate has been lowered (Naidu & Oliver, 1996; Frankola, 2001). In the period Fall 1997 through Fall 1999, UMUC's Web-based courses in its Graduate School of Management and Technology (7275 enrollments) had a 10.6% non-completion rate, as compared with 7% in conventional classrooms (Shayne, 2000). Later studies of undergraduates have also shown a larger withdrawal rate from online courses than from face-to-face courses: in one semester 13% vs. 10% and in a summer semester 29% vs. 8%. Overall, the undergraduate withdrawals averaged 24% online vs. 12% face-to-face. The causes of these differences are yet to be adequately pinned down. The larger differences between the Frankola findings, which are more representative of higher education generally, and those of UMUC are also yet to be explained. (Sheckley, 2000; on causes of withdrawals, see also Kashy, 1997; Kashy, Thoennessen, Thai, Davis & Wolfe, 1997).

The case from the New Jersey Institute of Technology (NJIT) in 1997 presented the students' perspective on efficiency (Hiltz, 1997). NJIT had two complete undergraduate degree programs available through a mix of video plus Virtual Classroom (an asynchronous, computer conferencing system)—the B. A. in Information Systems and the B. S. in Computer Science. Due to institutional budget cuts, NJIT's working, first-generation college students were faced with overcrowded classes that filled up and closed quickly. Since these technical degree programs have rigid sequences of courses that must be taken in order, being closed out of a pre-requisite course any given semester could significantly lengthen the students' time to degree. The distance learning sections provided another option. The intensive interaction and support available online via these dual technologies also enabled more motivated students to proceed at an accelerated pace. Thus, the distance learning option saved NJIT students time and money in their progress toward degree completion.

While these cases and statistics argue well for MI/DL's potential to enhance access, retention, and progress toward the degree, there is still the danger of leaving some student populations behind by our choice of technology, course design, and student supports. Without adequate opportunity for individual student-faculty interaction or peer study groups, for example, the Teletechnet model would not be attractive to some learners. Similarly, computer conferencing (and most current Web-based learning) is heavily dependent on writing and availability of computer technology. A learner coming back to school with poor skills, a need for structure or the motivation provided by personal relationships, and without a home computer may find as many obstacles to learning via the new technologies as those confronted in coming to campus. Many campuses experimenting with online coursework are finding that the majority of their enrollees are their own on-campus students. Thus, we may not be meeting the needs of those learners who currently have the least access.

RESTRUCTURING CLASSES AND RETHINKING PEDAGOGY

Most faculty continue to view the instructional possibilities of distance learning in terms of their past experiences with the classroom. For this reason video-based modes are heavily dependent on the lecture and text, and the Web is used primarily as a publishing medium. In many cases teachers have not kept pace with changes in digital communication technologies—especially within the Web environment—that have changed the potential of technology-mediated instruction. These technological advances coincide with teaching reforms that emphasize strategies such as problem solving, collaborative learning, mastery learning, experience and reflection—strategies aligned with the very learning principles discussed throughout this book.

The Rensselaer Polytechnic Institute "studio" classes have been mentioned previously as a model for using technology in a whole new pedagogical framework that enhances learning outcomes (Wilson, 1994, 1997). The RPI goal was to reduce lecture time, better integrate laboratory experiences and technology, incorporate more hands-on learning, and emphasize collaborative learning throughout a course. This case also illustrated the benefit of utilizing existing instructional materials to keep development costs down. Proven introductory Physics materials were utilized at the computer workstations of the workshop facility. The typical configuration of large lecture and teaching assistant-led labs was changed to classes of about 50 taught by a team of one faculty member, one graduate student, and one or two undergraduates. Despite the fact that class contact time was reduced by one third, students learned the material better and faster (Wilson, 1994, 1997).

Although Rensselaer's studio classes are on-campus, a similar environment has been established for distance learners in other courses. In these cases, classes are primarily asynchronous, but 10-20% of the course activity is synchronous, incorporating discussion, small group projects, and role-playing. The multimedia learning environment has the following characteristics:

- Delivery on standards-based multimedia PCs equipped for live video/audio interactions and connected to a robust multi-casting network.
- A mix of synchronous and asynchronous activity.
- Use of Web- and/or CD-ROM-based multimedia materials.
- Use of professional quality software tools for CAD, symbolic math, spreadsheets, word processing, etc.
- Live audio and/or video interactions among the students and with faculty.
- E-mail interactions among the students and faculty.

- Small group discussions.
- Collaborative software for application sharing over the network.
- Access to rich resources on the network.
- Ability to "pass the floor" to students to allow them to lead the class through an activity.
- Course administration software to track student progress.

A somewhat different approach, based on mastery learning, is demonstrated in introductory Physics classes at Michigan State University (Kashy et al, 1997a; 1997b). A re-design of a 500-student calculus-based physics course for engineers, this case was part of the SCALE study by University of Illinois, Urbana-Champaign, funded by Sloan Foundation. The tools consist of an Asynchronous Learning Network (ALN) for student assistance and of a networked software system to implement a Computer-Assisted Personalized Approach (CAPA) for assignments, quizzes, and examinations. The use of technology permits a reallocation of instructors' and teaching assistants' time, shifting it from tasks such as grading and record keeping to direct student help. The course was organized without recitation sections, thereby reducing staffing needs. Only 66% of the previous staff was required for the ALN and the Physics Learning Center where students obtain online and face-to-face help respectively. Even the traditional lecture time is now used to integrate student exercises and discussion.

At the same time, the newly designed course raised standards in learning outcomes. Students were expected to demonstrate higher order conceptual understanding in addition to manipulation of formulae. In the revised format about one third of every exam deals with concepts—not numerical calculations. Unlike some computerized assignment systems, CAPA is well suited to conceptual questions and problems. The system also enables teaching staff to identify students at risk early on and provide mentoring. In past studies, similar individualized computer-based learning systems have consistently reduced learning time by one third (Keeton & Sheckley, 1997). To further enhance and speed learning, faculty and teaching assistants focus on helping students discover the *mis*conceptions they have in their mental maps about the subject. In MSU's experience, the instant feedback and opportunity to resubmit assignments with errors corrected, along with the opportunity to seek and obtain one-on-one help in flexible ways has resulted in improved student performance on exams, a lower drop-out rate, and a higher standard of learning outcomes.

Although one model above is based on collaborative learning and the other on mastery learning, their pedagogical features and the underlying learning principles are very much the same. Each format:

- Engages students as active learners, not passive recipients of knowledge.
- Gives continuous and immediate feedback, with computer tracking of student activity, so that instructor knows when/how/where to intervene.

- Facilitates group discussion and peer interaction.
- Provides continuous assessment.
- Links multiple rich representations of phenomena.
- Develops technical skills important for life and workplace success.
- Uses hands-on tools and problems, while encouraging students to work collaboratively.
- Accommodates students with different learning styles (multisensory vs. linear).

INTERACTIVITY AND THE PROMISE OF NEW TECHNOLOGIES

Course designs differ considerably in the ways in which they encourage interaction, and thus active learning. Most student time—whether in traditional classes or technology-mediated instruction—is spent interacting with the subject matter through media that simulate a guided conversation with another person. All well-designed teaching materials—textbooks, study guides, and computer-assisted instruction—are interactive in this sense (Bates, 1997). Other definitions of interactivity stipulate that the action involves intrinsic feedback; i.e., the information in the system changes as a result of the students' action (Laurillard, 1993). Ideally, teaching is adaptive and reflective. In this definition hypertext, for example, is not interactive, while an intelligent computer tutor is.

Our learning principles and the empirical evidence on which they are based, however, demonstrate learning to be a social activity (Flavell, Miller et al., 1993). Videoconferencing, audio conferencing, and computer conferencing can provide human interaction with the originator of the teaching materials, a tutor who mediates between the material and other students.[2]

The great potential of Web-based instruction, in either its synchronous or asynchronous conversation formats, lies in the fact that the learning materials are close at hand and readily available, thus allowing interactions with others about the materials to be both convenient and immediate. Many observers have also pointed out that even the necessity of writing responses adds a more reflective element than is usually found in face-to-face interaction (Morihara, 1999). As audio and video infuse the Web course environment, instructors will soon have options within computer conferencing that include natural synchronous and asynchronous human dialogue.

It is within these dialogues that important learning takes place—especially the development of higher order thinking skills and the development of metacognition crucial to the expert learner (Lin, Newby et al. 1994; Flavell, Miller & Miller, 1993). It is here that human interaction over a period of time can accommodate the differences between individual learners in a highly personal conversation. The interaction, however, must promote certain processes and the instructor must be trained to

---

2 Correspondence study, of course, includes some interaction with an instructor via comments on returned assignments; however, this feedback is usually not a dialogue and is very delayed. The high dropout rate of such study is commonly attributed to lack of interactivity and the motivation it provides.

facilitate these processes (Schraw 1998). Marton and Ramsden (1988) present several recommendations for teaching which serve as a guide for maximizing learning through student-instructor interaction and student-student interaction.

1. Present the learner with new ways of viewing information and problems.
2. Focus on a few critical issues and show how they relate.
3. Integrate substantive and syntactic structures.
4. Make the learners' conceptions explicit to them.
5. Highlight the inconsistencies within and the consequences of learners' conceptions.
6. Create situations where learners center attention on relevant data.
7. Test students' understanding of phenomena; use the results for diagnostic assessment and curriculum design.
8. Use reflective teaching strategies.

In particular, items 4, 5, 7, and 8 describe the kind of interaction that enables an instructor to understand a student's mental model and then prescribe how the interaction should continue thereafter. (See also Garrison, 1987.) Marton & Ramsden (1988) also suggest that students' views be represented and taken into account in the approach to teaching and assessment within the conferencing dialogue. Will computers with artificial intelligence ever be able to provide this kind of interactivity? Will they have the same effect on student motivation? That remains to be seen. In the meantime, we cannot assume that the automated feedback or assessment possible in computer-based environments means we can dispense with human interaction. (We shall see that this question has obvious implications for cost savings.)

Choosing Technologies to Maximize Learning

Key to maximizing learning online is that the teacher be clear as to what is to be learned in each particular lesson and course, that the objectives be teased out with each goal in operationally clear terms, and that technologies then be chosen that best facilitate the students' development of the sought-after knowledge, skills, attitudes, habits or capabilities that combine these elements. In a project supported in part by the then Bell Atlantic Foundation, UMUC staff, led by Cynthia Whitesel, spelled out a seven-step process for clarifying learning objectives and matching each to an appropriate facilitating technology. For each learning activity (e.g., mastering concepts, problem solving, object and document analysis, data gathering and synthesis, case studies, virtual labs and field trips, presentations, collaborative learning, and authentic inquiry) four to six examples from actual practice are described. The examples come from 35 different educational institutions and were carried out by some 50 different instructors.

In a further module the project report discusses what is involved in using each of fifteen different technologies ranging from easy-to-use to hard-to-use. The technologies include animated graphics, other animations, applets, asynchronous communication, authoring programs, databases, downloaded media, images, repositories, scripts, streaming media, synchronous communication, text (html, pdf), web-based Power Point, and web sites. These aids to best use of the diverse technologies can be accessed at *http://www.edu/virtualteaching/module1/systems.html* for the teaching activities and a second module (insert "module 2" for "module 1") for the technologies (Whitesel, 1999).

ACHIEVING COST EFFECTIVENESS

In the cases above, institutions targeted courses with large annual enrollments and high risk of student failure or high unmet demand—a strategy that is more likely to result in reducing instructional costs, or at least holding costs constant. In each of these cases, cost savings in labor (in the form of either reductions in the number of instructors needed, or, more often, changes in the configuration of faculty and teaching assistants) offset up-front development costs and capital expenditures. Briefly, the cost side of each of the cases is sketched below.

Old Dominion University.   For Old Dominion's early downlink sites (including 15 receiving dishes, 10 transmittal classrooms, five computer labs, and library technology), the capital investment was $12,284,000. The imputed annual cost was almost one million dollars. When the system was operating at full capacity, annual system operating expenses for Teletechnet were $7,300,000 and the annual personnel costs were $12,295,000. For the four bachelor's degree programs on Virginia's community college campuses, these expenses included 72 full-time faculty, 12 part-time faculty, 70 professional support staff, 60 classified staff, and 20 hourly staff. The total cost on a course unit basis was $41,189. (The figure included $1,999 of the imputed capital costs.) The case compared this cost to that of (a) sending instructors around the state and (b) simply delivering conventional classes on Old Dominion's campus. With high demand courses the cost per student FTE was comparable between the Teletechnet and classroom delivery, while sending instructors statewide represented a cost that was 3.3 times higher. In low enrollment courses, the cost advantage went to the on-campus delivery. Given the relatively high fixed direct costs of Teletechnet and its low incremental cost per additional student, it can be expected to provide a cost advantage for large enrollment courses. Some years ago when Teletechnet was operating at 23% of planned capacity, its per course costs were about 27% higher than those projected; however, even at these levels, the system compared favorably with classroom costs for high demand courses (California State University System, 1999 January).

University of Illinois at Urbana-Champaign. The Spanish 210 ALN course was developed by a single faculty member over a summer and fall semester. The SCALE grant of $15,336 was divided roughly evenly between faculty summer support and student programming support. Since the professor had already authored online materials for her Italian courses, she was able to derive much of the Spanish 210 from it, thus saving development time. The increase in students per section noted resulted in significant savings, so that development costs were recouped within one semester. No additional delivery expenses, such as technical support for students, were detailed in UIUC's report (Arvan, Ory, Bullock, Burnaska & Hanson, 1998).

Rensellaer Polytechnic Institute. The changes of the new RPI program in number of sections, contact time and instructional staff resulted in cost savings in delivering the sections. The approximately 700 students enrolled in the large courses were divided into 12-15 sections of 48-64 persons. Where there had been 57-72 events to be staffed, there were now 12-15. Instructional time was reduced from six to four contact hours per week. Each section's team included two undergraduates. RPI budgeted capital costs of $100,000 for a 50-seat classroom with fixed computer stations—$1500 per seat and additional monies for any changes to ingress/egress, HVAC, wiring, lighting, and the like. (A room with adequate infrastructure re-purposed for laptops brought by the students could cost under $15,000.) Estimates of cost savings attributed to the Studio Classroom approach ranged from $10,000-$250,000 every time these Physics courses are taught. RPI has applied the same model to Calculus and Chemistry (Wilson, 1997b; Pipes & Wilson, 1996).

A joint Master's Degree in social work at Cleveland State University and the University of Akron (California State University System, 1999 February) illustrates another model with cost implications. Both institutions have had large undergraduate social work programs and wanted to establish the Master of Social Work degree. State policy, however, precluded establishing two such professional programs within less than 50 miles of each other. Furthermore, neither school had the financial resources to establish a full program. To resolve this dilemma the program was delivered via videoconferences, with each site originating half of the classes. Each campus financed a studio classroom for approximately $100,000 (with a useful life of four years); so, the operating budget for the joint program included an annual capital cost of $50,000. Each campus also hired three new full-time faculty members to fulfill the Continuing Social Work Education accreditation requirement of six positions. The total estimated cost of the joint program was over one million dollars, with a cost per student of $12,087. The cost of two separate programs (without, of course, the capital or annual technology expenditures) was projected to be $1,589,600, or $18,484 per student. The cost of one program on one campus—with reasonable projections of the decreased enrollment expected—was estimated at $651,660, or $14,684 per student.

Although it is too early in the life of the Western Governor's University (WGU) to evaluate its results, the model has certainly captured the imagination of the press and the higher education field. The cost effectiveness of WGU's concept is clear: this new breed of university promises to develop and offer assessment of competencies—a credentialing function rather than a teaching function, as already practiced by Excelsior College (formerly Regents College) of New York and Thomas Edison College of New Jersey. Instead of delivering its own courses, WGVU provides for the online distribution of other institution's curricula to its students. The college provides complete student services online as well. At least three features of the WGVU embody possible future directions with significant cost implications: the unbundling of educational functions; the focus on documenting competency, rather than seat time in courses; and the commercial partnerships with both the corporate sector and higher education (UCEA Annual Conference, 1999).

One can imagine other ways in which collaboration among more traditional institutions could diminish the very real fixed costs that usually accompany the use of mediated instruction. Whether an institution uses a single-faculty approach to course development or a team approach, course design time and costs could be reduced by using already-developed "instructional activities" within a discipline prepared by other institutions or sources. The use of already developed modules, problems, exercises, simulations and the like can shorten the time, introduce creative uses of the technology, and still enable individual faculty and departments to offer their own unique course on the subject.

Institutions could also collaborate on faculty training and course development. UMUC and the University System of Maryland were providing in 1999 a two-year "Web Initiative in Teaching" to sister institutions in the Maryland system. Teams of faculty and technical staff from each campus participated during the summer in two intensive weeks of workshops on Web pedagogy and course design. Participants followed up this training during the academic year by devoting one day per month to peer review, professional development, online interaction in asynchronous conferences, or piloting and assessing new courses. Cost savings can also be achieved via a multi-campus course development in those areas where the low enrollment at any single institution makes the up-front costs an obstacle for any single institution. Following this model UMUC is currently (2000-2001) extending its team-based centralized course development model to other institutions in Maryland in a collaboration called *MarylandOnline*. This model will cut development time in half for partner institutions, improve course design, and enable institutions to share delivery of more specialized, low-enrollment courses online. A joint project of 20 Maryland colleges with the support of the Maryland Higher Education Commission has undertaken to provide over training events within two years for 3000 faculty members in the use of technologies in teaching.

The IMS (Instructional Management Systems) project at EDUCAUSE, the MERLOT project at the California State University Center for Distributed Learning, and a FIPSE-funded project at Santa Barbara City College also hold promise for enhancing mediated instruction while cutting development costs (California State University System 1997 October and 1999 February 9, EDUCOM). All foster creation of "instructional activities"—multi-media simulations, problem-solving exercises, and the like—to be stored in accessible, standardized repositories for faculty. These may then be easily incorporated into a web-based environment for either distance or classroom learning. (Further, IMS standards define the technical specifications for interoperability of applications and services in distributed learning and support the incorporation of the IMS specifications into product and services worldwide. The latest specifications address basic functionality of labeling and finding content, moving content from one place to another, running content, and tracking student performance data.) It is hoped that these easily retrievable and re-useable chunks of content will save faculty time and save money for colleges.

COST CONTROVERSY

Policy papers (Twigg, 1996; Johnstone, 1996; Massey & Zemsky, 1995) that claim the new technologies are higher education's primary avenue to productivity usually rest their vision on "economies of scale." They assume one or more of the following: (1) all technologies have cost structures similar to video-based or print-based distance learning instruction; (2) mediated instruction means that instructor mediation is largely dispensable or can readily use lower-cost labor; (3) additional student support or technical support is minimal; (4) the life of software/courseware can be imputed over 8-30 years; and (5) there is little, if any cost, in training faculty.

Although the cases discussed above often do present savings with respect to high enrollment classes, the extent to which economies of scale create cost efficiencies varies considerably according to the technology and its particular application. Each technology has a different combination of development and fixed costs to delivery and variable costs—what Bates (1997) calls "cost structure." The lowest production cost is that for a conventional lecture classroom; the highest cost is that for pre-programmed computer-based learning or computer-controlled videodisc. Computer-mediated communication and print fall in the middle range. Likewise, technologies differ as to the cost of delivery. Radio, for example, has zero delivery cost. CD-ROMs are very inexpensive to deliver compared to the cost of production. Video-conferencing costs generally go down the larger the audience. Web-based computer conferencing may be relatively inexpensive to develop (especially when relying on individual faculty with little support), but its delivery costs increase in proportion to the number of students, if levels of interactivity are maintained. So, its cost structure is not so conducive to savings through economies of scale.

The cases also point out that cost effectiveness is often achieved through a change in instructional staffing (i.e., allowing the computer to mediate some or all instruction instead of the instructor, and/or utilizing large numbers of teaching assistants or undergraduate peer mentors/tutors instead of faculty). (See also CSU System, 1999 January 25, Virginia Tech.) Since we have seen the importance of interaction—student-faculty interaction as well as student-student interaction—this change cannot be inconsequential. We know that faculty report spending more time (due to student interaction) teaching Web-based courses than conventional ones (UMUC 2000), unless automatic grading and record-keeping can be largely assumed by the system or other staff provide students online help. We have little empirical evidence, however, to inform our choices about staffing, based on educational benefits.

In the few detailed cost-effectiveness studies on distance education, additional costs for student services support and student technical support are not usually specified. Yet, we know these elements are essential to higher student satisfaction and completion. Likewise, faculty support is given little attention in the studies. The Teaching, Learning, and Technology affiliate of the American Association of Higher Education (TLT Group)(Gilbert, 2001) documents the extreme understaffing of technical support resources on campuses attempting to integrate the new technologies into instruction. To orient faculty not only to the technology, but to effective pedagogy requires an infrastructure of staffing that includes instructional designers, graphics and media specialists, Web designers, and trainers.

Finally, studies often impute the life of courseware over eight or more years. In fact, at UMUC courses require revision every two to three years. The life of Web-based and other technologically-mediated courses is shortest in the more technical graduate-level courses of study. Few campuses have systematic development-revision cycles at this point, but those policy-makers who predicate higher education's future productivity on the new technologies must recognize a need for course revision that, like course creation, goes beyond the individual faculty member's time.

In 1999 FIPSE funded the Western Interstate Consortium for Higher Education (WICHE) to develop a costing methodology for the use of technology. Their work enables institutions to plan the use of mediated instruction by calculating real costs over time, rather than viewing use of technology as an added cost to existing courses or an inexpensive way to deliver new courses and garner new enrollments. The Technology Costing Methodology (TCM) project has produced three useful items available online: a handbook that outlines the policies and methodologies for calculating technology costs; a casebook that describes pilot implementation case studies; and a tabulator, an EXCEL spreadsheet for implementing the handbook procedures. The URL is *http://www.wiche.edu/telecom/projects/tcm/proj-products.htm*.

Concluding Note

Neither the cost effectiveness studies on productivity nor the MI/DL research on learning effectiveness provide an adequate assessment of distance education from the point of view of our definition of efficiency. Prior discussions have focused on managerial strategies from the institution's perspective. None of the models take into account the higher order of learning outcomes, the savings of *student* time and money, or the enhanced student learning evidenced in several of this book's case studies. The new technologies provide a relatively uncharted opportunity to combine both the managerial strategies and the learning principles presented here.

The new technologies will make it increasingly difficult to justify continuing a system of delivery (whether face-to-face or traditional distance education) that is expensive and ineffective for great segments of our society. Just as clearly the new technologies will only *increase* higher education's focus on methods of teaching and learning that match the uses of technology with the needs of learners in the twenty-first century. In this forecast, Tony Bates (1997) rightly places the emphasis, still, on the teacher and learner:

> . . . developments in multimedia that give teachers and learners the tools to re-construct and personalize knowledge, the development of computer-mediated communications, and the integration of multimedia with electronic networks suggest that the essential function of computers in education is moving away from the notion of the computer as substitute teacher towards that of 'true' technology, a set of tools to be used by teachers and learners to facilitate the task of learning and understanding (page 227).

REFERENCES

Arvan, L. (1997, March). The economics of ALN: Some issues. *Journal of Asynchronous Learning Networks 1*(1), [On-line]. 11pp. Available: *http://www.aln.org/alnweb/journal/issue1/arvan.htm* [1999, January 7]

Arvan, L., Ory, J. C., Bullock, C. D., Burnaska, K. K., & Hanson. M. (1998, September). The SCALE efficiency projects. *Journal of Asynchronous Learning Networks 5:* (7) [On-line]. 28 pp. Available: (*http://www.firstmonday.dk/issues/issue3_1/noble*)

Bates, A. W. (1997). *Technology, open learning and distance education* (2nd ed.). London and New York: Routledge.

Berge, Z. (1997). Characteristics of online teaching on postsecondary, formal education. *Educational Technology, 37:* (3) 35-47.

California State University System (1999, January 5) *Case studies in evaluating the benefits and costs of mediated instruction and distributed learning.* 7pp, [Benefits of the human computer interaction program.] *http://www.calstate.edu/special_projects/mediated_instr/RSVP/benefits.html.*

California State University System (1999, January 5). *Case studies in evaluating the benefits and costs of mediated instruction and distributed learning.* 29pp. Available online at http://www.calstate.edu/special_projects/mediaed_instr/teletech. [Case of Old Dominion University and "two plus two" programs at community colleges in Virginia]

California State University System (1999, February 9). *Case studies in evaluating the benefits and costs of mediated instruction and distributed learning.* 11pp. Available online at *http://www.calstate.edu/special_projects/mediated_instr/Ohio/index.html.* [Case of the master's degree in social work at Cleveland State University and the University of Akron.]

California State University System (1997, October) *Case studies in evaluating the benefits and costs of mediated instruction and distributed learning.* Abstract and EDUCOM Panel on Case Study Results Oct. 1997 Power Point slides, [On-line], 38 pp. Available at *http://www.calstate.edu/special_projects/mediated_instr/Case_Studies.html* [1999, February 9].

California State University System (1999, January 25). *Case studies in evaluating the benefits and costs of mediated instruction and distributed learning, 21pp.* Available at *http://www.calstate.edu/special_projects/mediated_instr/Virginia/index.html.* [Course restructuring and the instructional development initiative at Virginia Polytechnic Institute and State University: A benefit cost study.].

Flavell, J. H., Miller, P. H., & Miller, S. A. (1993). Social cognition. In J. H. Flavell, P. H. Miller & S. A. Miller: *Cognitive development.* Englewood Cliffs, Prentice-Hall: 173-227.

Frankola, K. (2001, June). The e-learning taboo: High dropout rates in online courses. *Syllabus, 14*(11), 2pp.

Garrison, D. R. (1987, October-December). Self-directed and distance learning: Facilitating self-directed learning beyond the institutional setting. *International Journal of Lifelong Education, 6*(4).

Gilbert (2001). The TLT group. *http://www.tltgroup.org.* Washington, DC: AAHE

Haughey, M. & Anderson, T. (1998). *Networked learning: The pedagogy of the Internet.* Montreal: Cheneliere/McGraw-Hill.

Hazemi, R., Hailes, S., & Wilbur, S. (Eds.) (1998). *The digital university: reinventing the academy.* Berlin, New York: Springer.

Hiltz, S. R. (1997). Impacts of college-level courses via asynchronous learning networks: Some preliminary results. *Journal of Asynchronous Learning Networks.* [online], 11pp. Available: *http://eies.njit.edu/~hiltz/workingpapers/philly/philly.htm.*

Hiltz, S. R. & Turoff, M. (2000). ALN Evaluation. *Sixth International Conference on Asynchronous Learning Networks,* November 3-5. Adelphi, MD: UMUC.

Institute for Higher Education Policy (1999). *What's the difference? A review of contemporary research on the effectiveness of distance education in higher learning.* Washington, DC: 1-42.

Johnstone, D. B. (1996). Learning productivity: A new imperative for American higher education. *NLII Viewpoint, 1*(1). [On-line]. 16pp. Available: *http://www. educom.edu/program/nlii/articles/johnstone.html* [1999, January 7]

Jonassen, D. H. & Reeves, T. C. (1996). Learning with technology: Using computers as cognitive tools. In D.H. Jonassen (Ed.): *Handbook of research for educational communications and technology* (pp. 693-719). New York: Simon & Schuster Macmillan.

Kashy, E., Thoennessen, M., Tsai, Y., Davis, N. E., & Wolfe, S. L., (1997). Using networked tools to enhance student success rates in large classes. *Proceedings of the Frontiers in Education.* [On-line]. Available: *http://fairway.ecn.purdue.edu/~fie/fie97/papers/1046.pdf*

Kashy, E., Thoennessen, M., Tsai, Y., Davis, N. E., & Wolfe, S. L., (1997). Application of technology and asynchronous learning networks in large lecture classes. In Jay F. Nunamaker, Jr. (Ed.): *31st Hawaii International Conference on System Sciences 1. Collaboration Systems and Technology Track.* page 321.

Laurillard, D. (1993). *Rethinking university teaching: A framework for the effective use of educational technology.* London and New York: Routledge.

Lin, X., & T. J. Newby, et al. (1994). *Embedding metacognitive cues into hypermedia systems to promote far transfer problem solving.* National Convention of the Association for Educational Communications and Technology. Nashville.

Marton, F., & Ramsden, P. (1998). What does it take to improve learning? In P. Ramsden (Ed.): *Improving learning: New perspectives.* London: Kogan Page.

Massey, W. F. & Zemsky, R. (1995). Using information technology to enhance academic productivity, [On-line}.

Morihara, B. B. (1999). University web teaching practice and pedagogy. Unpublished dissertation, Oregon State University.

Naidu, S. & Oliver, M. (1996). Computer-supported collaborative problem-based learning: An instructional design architecture for virtual learning in nursing education. *Journal of Distance Education, 11:* (2) 1-22.

Pipes, R. B. & Wilson, J.M. (1996). A multimedia model for undergraduate education. *Technology in Society, 18:* (3) 387-401.

Porter, L. R. (1997). *Creating the virtual classroom: Distance learning with the Internet.* New York: John Wiley & Sons.

Potter, C. (1998). Towards open learning: The combination of lecturing, student-led tutorials and distance education techniques in large-group university teaching. Improving University Learning and Teaching, Dublin.

Roblyer, M. D., Edwards, J., & Havriluk, M.A. (1997). *Integrating educational technology into teaching.* Upper Saddle River, NJ: Prentice-Hall.

Russell, T. L. (1999). *The no significant difference phenomenon.* Chapel Hill, NC: Office of Instructional Telecommunications, North Carolina State University.

Schraw, G. (1998). On the development of adult metacognition. In M. C. Smith & T. Pourchot, (Eds.): *Adult learning and development: Perspectives from educational psychology.* Mahwah, Lawrence Erlbaum Associates: 89-106

Shayne, V. (2000). Student course withdrawal as a function of participation in online and face-to-face courses, IRAHE Research Papers, June 30. Adelphi, MD: UMUC.

Sheckley, B. G. (2000). A comparison of student withdrawals in online and face-to-face BMGT courses, Fall 1997 through Spring 2000. December. *IRAHE Studies.* Adelphi, MD: UMUC.

Twigg, C., (1996). Academic productivity: The case for instructional software. A Report from the Broadmoor Roundtable. Colorado Spring, Colorado, July 24-25, 1996, [On-line] 26 pp. Available: *http://www.educause.edu/nlii/keydocs/broadmoor.html* [1999, January 7] UCEA 1999 Annual Conference. Washington D.C., April, 1999.

Whitesel, C. (1999). *Systems approach to designing online learning activities.* Available at *http://www.umuc.edu/virtualteaching/module1/systems.html* and *http://www.umuc.edu/virtualteaching/module2/systems.html.* Adelphi, MD: UMUC

Wilson, J. M. (1994, December). The CUPLE physics studio. *The Physics Teacher, 32,* 518.

Wilson, J. M. (1997a). How computing and communications are changing physics education. From International Conference on Undergraduate Physics Education, 1996, College Park, MD. In E.F. Ridish & J. S. Rigden (Eds.), *The Changing Role of Physics Departments in Modern Universities,* 357-373. Woodbury, NY: The American Institute of Physics.

Wilson, J. M. (1997b, July). Studio teaching: When the future becomes the present. *UniServe Science News, 7,* 3-5.

CHAPTER 10

Support Instruction with More Efficient Administration

Colleges and universities today can gain in effectiveness and efficiency by using a combination of tactics to implement an overall strategy suited to the distinctive mission of an institution. A set of tactics educators might use to create an efficient institution of higher education could include:

- supporting faculty and students in applying the key learning principles discussed in Chapters 1-8,
- making optimal use of the new technologies for communication and instruction as discussed in Chapter 9,
- striving for still more efficient use of time of personnel, and
- structuring all policies and practices to enhance achievement of the institution's educational mission.

As we will explain, the efficiency of which we write here is not that of merely reducing the costs of instruction per semester hour but also emphasizing and pressing for efficiency in facilitating substantial gains in students' learning.

We have in this book recounted stories of teachers' and colleges' enhancing students' learning in ways that contain or reduce the direct costs of courses and programs of study. With the aid of these stories and the probing of published research on learning, we have identified eight principles underlying these efficiencies. In closing, we turn to experiences in the efforts to *gain efficiency in whole institutions* and to examples of both strategies and tactics that managers of educational institutions can use to complement the efforts of faculty and students.

EFFICIENT INSTITUTIONS OF LEARNING

No two of the efficient institutions highlighted in our discussions have achieved efficiency in the same way. Using principles we advocate, each of the institutions has saved time and money for both itself and the learners it serves while also enhancing the learning students achieved. Some of the featured institutions cater to working adults only, some to students of traditional college-going age, some to both older and younger students, and some to employees in a business setting.

We have dealt in detail with applying Principles 1 through 8 in the preceding chapters. Before speaking to the other strategies introduced in this chapter, we use the examples of UMUC, Empire State College, Antioch College, IBM, and Alverno College to illustrate the diversity of ways in which common principles can work for efficiency in learning. Following this discussion we turn to a further clarification of how institution-wide strategies can be employed to achieve efficiency in learning.

MANY WAYS TO EFFICIENCY IN LEARNING

To repeat a main theme of this chapter, colleges and universities have found numerous ways of achieving efficiency. For example, UMUC combines six strategies to enhance learning while lowering costs:

- use of practitioner-faculty as adjunct instructors,
- a customer service emphasis that offers classes and support services at times and locations that are convenient for students,
- focus in the curriculum upon majors (fields of study) that interest large numbers of working adults,
- extensive use of communications technologies,
- assessment of non-credentialed college-level learning in terms of academic credit or advanced standing, and
- partnerships in which employers of students contribute facilities and communications services (Porosky, 1999).

Each of these elements either enhances the opportunities for students to learn or saves costs to the institution and its students. The use of adjunct faculty, for example, does both. Perhaps because more than 85% of UMUC students work full time (Wisan, 2000), they consistently report that they learn best from faculty who are practitioners in the fields in which they teach. The University chooses practitioners with the best academic credentials and with a primary motivation to teach. It then provides orientation, training in the use of the new technologies, an occasional listserv (online discussion group), and frequent workshops on teaching. Such faculty are more cost effective because they spend their UMUC time almost entirely on teaching, not committee work or research (Porosky, 1999).

Beginning in the mid-1990s UMUC experienced a rapid growth in online course enrollments. They reached almost 40,000 course enrollments in the academic year 1999-2000 and almost 60,000 in the academic year 2000-2001. This trend is noteworthy in showing the University's rapid integration of innovations into its overall strategy to achieve effectiveness and efficiency in providing instruction that is affordable, academically sound, and conveniently accessible (Porosky, 1999).

In the early 1990s Empire State College (ESC) achieved costs per student per year that were lower by more than 20% than similar costs for other State University of New York (SUNY) members (Keeton, 1999b). Each working adult who attends ESC is assigned a mentor who works with the student to develop an individualized degree contract. Within a state-mandated degree design the mentor-mentee team then develops "sub-contracts" for components of that degree plan. A component might be a tutorial with a specialist, an independent study project, a training sequence at the student's worksite, or a course taken in another university. The mentor combines the roles of academic adviser, coach, instructor (if the student does a tutorial with the mentor), and a supervisor of program quality for the student. There is no separate student service staff. The need for ESC-owned facilities is minimal.

Like UMUC, ESC offers distance education options. The ESC mentors act also as the prior learning assessment "instructors" for their mentees. The student may earn as much as the equivalent of 90 semester hours of credit through this service. Contrary to the common belief that individualization of instruction must be highly expensive, ESC has created a highly efficient way of applying this strategy (Keeton, 1999b).

Antioch College has, since 1920, used a single faculty and physical plant to serve two student bodies who alternate periods of study on campus with work off campus (Keeton, 1999a). Students work off-campus one term in diverse settings that require them to apply their skills and knowledge. In an alternating term they participate in classes on campus. These classes require students to question, reflect, and test theory against practices and experiences they have gained in their off-campus work—whether in courses on business management, ethics, composition, or the sociology of families. This interaction between experience and theory provides a powerful dynamic for further learning. The frugal use of faculty load, physical space, and time in classrooms results in a low relative cost for the outcomes in student maturation and learning. The Antioch of the 1990s is a university of five colleges, of which four are primarily for adult learners. These adult-centered institutions seek the yeastiness of the mother college by way of concurrent work and study rather than alternating periods (Keeton, 1999a).

Businesses as well as colleges and universities are deeply involved in educating today's workforce and face similar problems of achieving cost efficiencies in training and education. International Business Machines (IBM) had in the 1980s a widely-heralded human resource development program. As told by an external team, however, the firm itself questioned its own efficiency. In 1984 the cost of its employee education and training was almost $1 billion per year. After a two-year study, the company eliminated courses not important for productivity, undertook a substantial redesign of its training program and added to its assessment of the employees' learning. By 1989, IBM had moved half or more of its training from classrooms to self-paced instruction and planned to reduce classroom instruction to 25% of all training within a decade, thereby reducing its per student costs from $350 per day for classroom instruction to $75 per day for computer, video- or print-based independent study. By 1992 a paradigm shift had been accomplished. Increases had been achieved in both employee learning outcomes and in productivity (Twigg & Doucette, 1992).

Among colleges the concern for efficiency is critical for the instruction of traditional college-going students as well as for the growing adult clientele. Alverno College, serving primarily women of traditional college-going age, but now also enrolling working women (in its weekend college), has developed over a quarter of a century a bachelor's degree program designed to develop eight major competencies in its students. As spelled out in the stories in earlier chapters drawn from IRAHE case studies, Alverno has made exemplary use of learning principles, in part by an unusual practice of scheduling faculty's Friday afternoons for work on the curriculum, instruction, and in-house research on them (Bowne & Engelmann, 1999; Mente, 1999; Witkowski & Magness, 1999).

Finding a Grand Strategy to Fit Institutional Mission

An institution of higher education needs an overall strategy that is congruent with its primary educational mission. Where missions differ, the overall strategies need to reflect those differences. Institutions of higher education in the United States are more diverse in their missions than those of any other country. We have community colleges, liberal arts colleges of various degrees and types of selectivity, research universities and comprehensive universities, and universities of different degrees of "comprehensiveness." With the advent of distance education technologies, the diversity has further expanded. Additionally, as institutions adapt to changes influencing their operations (e.g., initiating distance education programs), they do not always stay with their initial choice of mission nor even with a state-mandated one.

As leaders of each type of institution face the challenges that accompany the new millenium (e.g., shifting demographics, new technologies, global economies) they strive to maximize the quality of their institution's performance within its stated mission while doing so at the most favorable cost. In the examples cited above, each institution had a distinctive mission and a grand strategy congruent with that commitment.

The triple goal we address in advocating efficiency is to enhance learning outcomes, to cut costs to both students and their institutions, and to do so without adding to the workload of faculty. The aim is not merely to contain costs (i.e., to reduce them, to arrest the rate of their increase, or to hold them constant in a given year's dollars). Nor is it simply to get better results with less rapidly rising costs, commendable as that goal is.

The goal is not just to save costs for the education provider (college, university, employer) without also lowering them for the student, nor vice versa. In pursuing the goal of efficiency in university operations, educators sometimes equate efficiency with cost-cutting alone. In doing so they can lose sight of the fact that when cost-cutting compromises or fails to enhance students' learning, there is a net loss in efficiency in what the university is supposed to be doing; namely, furthering learning.

Efficiency in learning is not the same as efficiency in credit-production. The difference requires emphasis. Most productivity studies in higher education focus on costs per credit hour or costs per student degree earned (Hollins, 1992). Neither credit hours nor degrees are accurate measures of learning. We believe that the efforts of state legislatures, state higher education commissions, and employers to foster accountability will be misdirected until they adopt *learning outcomes* as the index to the benefits sought.

Historically the goals for college education in America have not been those given priority in this book; that is, the advancement of learning and personal development. Selection into the professions, provision of an opportunity to "grow up" in low-risk conditions, employability, and indoctrination into a value-orientation of the sponsors (e.g., religious or patriotic) have been among the primary purposes (Kraft, 1995). The focus urged here is upon learning and human development at an optimal ratio of benefits to costs.

We highlight now a choice of overall management strategies and tactics that, when interwoven with the teaching strategies already treated, can yield the quality and the efficiency we recommend. As our examples will show, the interweaving is not only important but is almost unavoidable in good practice.

ALTERNATIVE OVERALL STRATEGIES FOR LEARNING: AN OPTION

Colleges and universities today tend to have either no coherent overall strategy for enhancing students' learning or a flawed one. Among those without a coherent strategy, the prevailing pattern has been one of introducing many enhancements to learning without an integrating framework in the hope that the existing cost structures will accommodate innovations. Using this strategy, administrators chip away at the edges of many budgets in hopes of accumulating a large advantage. Thereafter, they complain of, and try to reduce, the resulting "administrative lattice," "academic ratchet," and "growth by accretion" (Zemsky & Massy in Hollins, 1992). Essentially, they are trying to "contain costs," not reduce them, within an unchanged basic framework for conducting instruction.

Twigg and Doucette (1992) describe how ineffective this strategy is when applied to the single area of using technology to enhance learning. Productivity will probably not be enhanced, they say, if no change of paradigm is made when new technology is adopted. Indeed, productivity may decrease because of its added cost. The pattern of sequential study delivered mostly face-to-face in classrooms, often in residential institutions that include complete lifestyle bundles might be called a Framework Inviting Inefficiency (FII) and can be summarized as follows:

1. learning activities are institution- and teacher-controlled;
2. education for which the college grants credentials occurs only or almost entirely in and around classrooms;
3. learning is interrupted when semesters end or when students stop out;

4. the discipline-oriented department is the optimal locus of control of curricular offerings and instructional assignments;
5. hands-on use of books and library resources is strongly emphasized;
6. learning is best done by students working alone;
7. surmounting external barriers to learning is the student's responsibility; and
8. the first responsibility of faculty is to transmit knowledge to students and in doing so to cover all material designated by the department.

Features 2, 3, 5, 6, 7, and 8 actually introduce inefficiency by slowing down or delaying learning while adding to costs of achieving desired results. Other features of the FII make it difficult to replace features that are defective. Normally some features of the FII are modified or abandoned, but this overall pattern continues to dominate American higher education.

ADOPTING AN EFFICIENT OVERALL STRATEGY

If a principal purpose of higher education today is to facilitate learning, the basic strategy for doing so should be one that assures the effectiveness and efficiency of the processes sketched in Chapters 1 through 8. *An alternative structure,* a Framework that supports Effectiveness and Efficiency (FEE) could be described as:

● continuous,
● controlled mainly by the learners,
● using the workplace and home as learning sites for learning,
● involving non-formal study as well as formal,
● employing technologies to help students access colleges from distant and dispersed sites,
● being supplemented by tailored, powerful support programs, and
● having all non-teaching services unbundled, easily accessible, and optional, designed to serve the learners.

In an FEE faculty work as mentors (coaches), expert resources, instructional designers, managers of learning services, and consultants to non-collegiate education providers (such as corporate human resource development centers).

The efficiencies reflected in the stories at the beginning of this chapter are more readily achievable within a framework that encourages efficiency. Both structures, FII and FEE, present great challenges to faculty members. Each, though, calls for different kinds of talent and performance. We do not intend to suggest that the FEE here sketched should be adopted by every college or university, but that each should follow the principles for enhancing learning that are outlined in this book. Like University of Maryland University College (Porosky, 1999) or Empire State College (Keeton, 1997b), colleges that use FEE will have built into their basic missions and structures an economy and productivity not achievable within the FII paradigm.

Tactics to Implement the FEE

GIVE PRIORITY TO THE EFFICIENT USE OF TIME

The most important single factor in cost-control in teaching and learning is time-saving. Why? Because the most expensive resource used in facilitating learning, relative to results gained, is the time of key persons: students, faculty, and those who support students' and faculty's work on the learning.

One might object that, in the new technologies for acquiring and manipulating information, the capital costs of hardware and software will outweigh personnel costs. As reported in Chapter 9, studies on this matter have shown that gains in efficiency via the new technologies were achieved primarily where enrollments were quite large, where they made possible savings in faculty time, or where they overcame access problems that otherwise imposed high per student costs. Over time we expect that the amortized costs of capitalization to particular institutions will be less than the ongoing costs to them of their users' time. This judgment has not yet, as far as we can learn, been firmly established. Whether it proves correct or not, once an institution has decided to use the technologies because of their power to enhance learning, the costs of time will then be the remaining key factor to heed.

Eliminate policies and procedures that waste students' time. Institutions interested in not wasting students' time can change or eliminate policies and practices that do so such as:

- failing to individualize the pacing of instruction (e.g., not allowing abler students to proceed at a faster pace than others or leaving slower learners "lost" or confused by a pace too rapid for them);
- preventing timely scheduling of students' courses by requiring inappropriate prerequisites, poor timing of course sequences, or both;
- requiring students to participate in courses that cover material they already know or seek to develop skills students already possess;
- repeating the same material in multiple courses beyond need for embedment of knowledge or skills;
- using inefficient methods of instruction (e.g., lecturing for outcomes better achieved in other ways);
- not capitalizing on the benefits that can be achieved through collaborative learning; and
- failing to use time-saving technologies.

Johnstone (1993) also lists ways in which tradition gobbles up the calendar or the day needlessly. For example, with adult students, timing of classes can be critically important. While evening and weekend colleges were a rarity a half-century ago, they are now common. No respectable institution of higher education today with a primary clientele of adult students would confine its offerings to weekday classes between 8:00 A.M. and 4:00 P.M. Working adults' calendars are *so diverse* no one time works best for all. Traditional daytime hours are best for some adults to attend classes, while the small hours of the morning work best for others, while other students may require some combination of hours (Aslanian & Brickell, 1980). Since adult students are concerned with the timing of course offerings as well as the amount of time required to complete the courses, the contemporary college or university must heed both in order not to impair students' effectiveness in use of their time.

Time can also be wasted by arrangements in the use of space. As with calendars and schedules, the contemporary university for adults who work must see to the most convenient location of classes, administrative services, and support services in order to conserve students' time and facilitate best timing of their use of services. Referring back to our discussion of UMUC (Porosky, 1999), a source of its efficiency for adult learners in Maryland is its close attention to this array of ways to save time and money through convenience of access to instruction (e.g., more than 30 course-delivery sites, multiple methods of delivering education at a distance, and dial-in registration and advisory services).

Develop ways to increase students' effective use of time. Beyond the ways to avoid wasting time listed above, another way to save time is to use one of three major strategies:

- *Cut the time used as each functional task is separately performed.* In the Rensselaer physics courses (Wilson, 1994) both teacher time and student time were saved by technology-assisted, collaborative learning with more active student use of studio problems. A simpler efficiency was achieved in the increased practice-and-feedback in the critical thinking course described in Chapter 2. Later such courses using special computer software realize even greater efficiencies.
- *Combine activities and accomplish them together.* Consider, for example, the approach to timely degree-completion used in the University of Connecticut's doctoral program in Adult Learning (Kehrhahn, Sheckley, & Travers, 2000). A program that has historically used an average of more than seven years for degree completers and that has had a high proportion of non-completers is now on the way toward an average of just over five years for completers and a higher proportion of completers. Why? The early clarification and negotiation of shared learning goals, task definitions, and marker events toward degree completion saved faculty time and costs per doctorate produced, enhanced the quality of the products of study (essays, recitations, dissertations), and shortened the elapsed calendar time required by students for degree completion. In short, time spent in degree completion is minimized while time-on-task is increased and made more productive. The factors yielding the efficiency are elements of the FEE.
- *Eliminate a step entirely.* For example, cut out lectures that merely convey knowledge that can be learned faster and more thoroughly with the aid of books,

videocassettes, or handouts (Kotler & Stonich, 1991). Well-designed lectures can still excite interest in learning, convey original ideas, facilitate critical reading, or meet other special needs but those that simply convey knowledge that can be accessed more efficiently can be eliminated.

We have documented earlier a number of tactics on time use that have succeeded in specific colleges. See, for example, the Alverno project combining from two courses into one work on reading and writing skills (Witkowski & Magness, 1999). This point is also illustrated by the University of Missouri-Kansas City strategy of pinpointing "high risk courses" and providing labor-saving tactics to the tutoring of students most endangered by the courses (Wilcox, 1999).

In higher education, the dimensions of quality (i.e., the benefits to stakeholders) include such matters as the scope of applicability of the knowledge or skills being gained, the extent to which durable skills or competencies, rather than quickly outdated ones, are learned, and the degree to which faculty elicit a deep desire for and enjoyment of learning among students. When students' time is saved and learning is made more enjoyable, these further dimensions of quality are more likely to be realized as well.

In reducing costs, use options that enhance learning. Cost reduction can be done in ways that are learning-neutral or even learning-negative in effect. Seeking out learning-enhancing options is the preferred strategy. For instance, among the 1100 or more colleges and universities that offer cooperative education (alternating or concurrent work and study) as a way of lowering net costs to students and to the institution, some institutions neglect to help students understand how to learn on the job. By pre-planning with a learning contract, obtaining cooperation of an immediate work supervisor, and following up with faculty debriefing the student on what was learned, a process that provided a student with some income and may have lowered a student's costs can also help to enhance a student's learning.

A great deal of work reported in research literature about improvement of teaching (e.g., use of problem-based learning as an alternative to lectures) (Barrow, 1994) is a matter of cost-neutral and learning-enhancement changes that departments and their faculties can make without affecting their budgets. As long as the work is within faculty load policies, any gain in learning that a change elicits will also be a gain in efficiency. Very little research, however, examines the combination of cost-cutting with learning gains or the combination of cost increases with demonstrably disproportionate gains in values realized.

Seek timely degree completion rather than time-shortened degrees. Comparison of the time-shortened degree with timely degree completion can clarify the task of saving time in reaching learning goals. The time-shortened degree has been a favorite among reformers for at least thirty years. According to Johnstone (1993), the movement began in the early 1970s with the Carnegie Commission Report, *Less Time,*

More Options, in which the Commission recommended shortening the Bachelors degree by one-year and the Masters degree and Ph.D. by one to two years. A number of time-shortened degree programs involving year-round study (e.g., in the California State University System) were tried, as well as programs coupling advanced study in high schools with more summer study (e.g., by Princeton University and George Washington University). Often these programs did not actually reduce students' hours in study, but crowded the same hours into fewer years by adding summer sessions. "For a variety of reasons, nearly all of these (and many other) programs failed to take hold..." (Johnstone, 1993, p. 29).

We favor, instead of a commitment to time-shortened degrees (even if *bona fide* time savers are included), the ideal of "timely degree completion." By stating this as an ideal we acknowledge that the most efficient process is not necessarily the shortest. In some cases a somewhat longer effort might yield a disproportionately more valuable outcome. By contrast, a number of measures commended by a 1994 SHEEO publication (Blanco, 1994), such as reducing credits required for degree and using year round study, may not yield learning gains at all.

One of the authors witnessed an example of speeding up achievement by slowing the pace at Union College in Schenectady, New York. Faced with adult learners matriculated in a rigorous engineering curriculum who were rusty or underprepared for calculus, the College provided more than a developmental non-credit option. The Mathematics Department created an alternative to the usual two-course college sequence, expanding it to three terms. Although this calculus sequence took students longer to earn the same number of credits, students were more likely to continue in the degree program and continue their introductory engineering science concurrently. Taking longer with calculus gave these part-time students a firm foundation for the rest of their degree program and increased their rate of completion.

Restructure Other Management Practices to Focus on the Educational Mission

A number of further tactics can help an institution to improve its administrative efficiency in ways compatible with its educational quality. We explore in this section ways to do so.

CUT DOWN ON INEFFICIENT ADMINISTRATIVE PRACTICES

While this book attends primarily to the improvement of instructional and learning efforts, these practices are always set in a context of administrative policies that may either conduce to their efficiency or work against it. For example, an Illinois Community College Board's Accountability Initiative in the early 1990s summarized many areas in which productivity initiatives were being undertaken (Hudgins,

1993). Most of these dealt with moves that can be taken administratively, eliminating unneeded programs and courses, arranging cooperation with other colleges in purchasing and delivery of other services including instruction, astute use of distance learning, interventions to increase student retention, improvements in registration systems, and elimination of needless red tape. Clearly such a plan identifying and eliminating inefficiencies should be a central component of any sensible strategy for efficiency. Total Quality Management (TQM) applications in higher education such as these have successfully enhanced administrative efficiency.

Choose Strategies for Net Efficiency, Not Just Cost Reduction

Risk of loss as well as promise of gain enters into the choice of strategies for institutional management and for enhancing learning. A focus only on cost reduction can jeopardize achieving optimal gains in students' learning. For example, in the financial management of institutions of higher education, the historic focus has more often been on risk avoidance than on optimizing gains. A substantial amount of the humor on college and university campuses today is devoted to the irrationalities of bureaucracy and red tape. A major administrator in one of the country's leading university systems recently summed up the situation as:

- Too many rules
- Too many signatures required
- 35% of the customers leave before they're done
- Too many meetings
- Meetings too inefficient
- Not enough clarity on priorities

Almost all of the regulations that elicit this satire were enacted for reasons that are still good. They focus, however, on managing risks associated with financial or educational mistakes (e.g., adding signatures to fix responsibility, adding meetings to avoid overlooking a key adviser's insights, risking a poor meeting to avoid planning time, or risking dropouts by saving time on helping students with barriers). In prescribing detailed rules and multiple monitors for a single transaction, these processes convert communities of highly talented and promising people into novice-like performers whose hands are tied by rules that they know are not best in many specific work situations (e.g., a requirement of multiple signatures for approval of travel already contracted for by the university). The day-to-day managers, however, do not dare let common sense override the fear that higher officers have of local, state, or other external bodies.

While the roles of government are under scrutiny in the interest of the nation's future, it would be most felicitous if states and boards of governors of institutions of higher education could find a way to combine integrity in management and its oversight with a primary focus upon the mission and purposes of the institutions.

Balance the Need for Resources Against Their Increased Costs

Another area for attention in achieving net efficiency in learning is that of balancing the need to enhance resources for learning accessible to students and faculty with the cost of increasing the resources and the ease of access to them. In the past there has been almost a direct correlation between the extent and quality of the resources (libraries, expert personnel) accessible to students on one hand and the annual costs of accessing them on the other hand. With the advent of the Internet and other means of communication with expert sources, this correlation can be reduced.

Seek New Ways of Building Community

In Chapter 8 we discussed the importance of an environmental press for inquiry—a culture of learning. That effort will be furthered if the climate is also one of collegiality and community. Forces in the outside world that work against such community and collegiality have become increasingly significant in the past two decades. Among the needs deriving from such outside forces are not only pressures to restrict inquiry on campuses but also widespread discomfort with issues of race and ethnicity or, more broadly, with issues of diversity among students and diversity of the family and cultural values that they bring to college. Of this matter Eaton (1991) says:

> The higher-education community should be experiencing some discomfort about race. . . . The discomfort should be associated with the limited extent to which minorities were successful and influential within the higher-education community, and the patronizing quality of higher-education activity such as special admission programs, the exploitation of athletes, and the complacency associated with enrolling just a few brightest and best minorities. The higher-education community should feel concerned about the gap between the rhetoric and the reality of minorities' availing themselves of higher education as a passage to a better life. The message for the 1990's is twofold: first, higher education clearly has been less than adequate in responding to the challenge of minority education, and second, the current state of separatism and polarization will not improve the situation (p. 162).

The idea of the college or university as a community of scholars and learners is an old and honored one, but increasingly felt to be honored more in the breach than in the observance. Researchers who study student retention report that "social integration" is a major factor in persistence to degree completion (Tinto, 1994; Pascarella & Terenzini, 1991). More recently, the pressure toward use of newer communications technologies to facilitate access to higher education and success in it have suggested a need for other approaches to the generation of community among students and teachers. Some research suggests that the student's sense of belonging in the university community and of acceptance as important within it may be even more critical to persistence than is "social integration" as earlier understood. (Dey & Hurtado, 1994). A fundamental need of colleges and universities is to have their people feel themselves as working together well in a vitally important shared enterprise.

MONITOR PROGRESS ON GOALS AND ADHERENCE TO STRATEGIES

Given a sound overall strategy, well-chosen goals, reasonably efficient administration, and an approach to enhancing learning by way of the institutional climate, the makeup of the institution, and rich resources for learning, a key need is to sustain these conditions by careful monitoring.

To monitor effectively, the goal(s) must be translated into measurable terms and monitored accordingly. Being clear about this goal of both enhancing students' proficiency and cutting costs to all parties calls for early clarification about the intended knowledge gains and skill and talent development that teachers and students seek and about the extent to which serendipitous gains in learning and maturity will be welcomed and facilitated. As colleges and universities have come to recognize that adults do a great deal of college level learning on their jobs, in volunteer activities (especially in leadership roles), and even in self-chosen reading, civic debates, and the like, the capacity to recognize and credit such learning and to place adults appropriately in the institution's curricular sequences has been greatly hampered by the lack of operationally clear statements by teachers about the outcomes they seek and realize in their normal classes.

Given the hesitancy in attacking the task of documenting learning outcomes, monitoring performance toward the goal is made even more difficult by lack of consensus within higher education or between it and the public about what to measure. Prather (1993), supporting the emerging demands, contends that outcomes, not processes, must be the medium of exchange in an acceptable accountability effort. "Common to all these reforms [to achieve accountability] is the argument that our institutions have lost sight of the outcomes they were created to produce and the customers they were supposed to [serve], and currently seek to be judged only on the basis of their methods or processes" (p. 51).

Agreement as to the most appropriate learning outcomes to be achieved is most difficult to realize: while colleges' catalogs *claim* that the years in residence yield good citizens and mature individuals, the teaching faculty normally demur and profess only to elicit greater knowledge, improved academic skills, and some capacity for higher order thinking. Proficiency in applying knowledge in discipline and profession is often neglected. The inventory of possible types of learning that compete for priority on that time include:

- *knowledge*: of data, concepts, methods of inquiry, history of a field of study, and advanced-level information in a discipline, profession or interdisciplinary area;
- *skills*: basic academic skills, work-related skills (basic, job-related, generic, and more advanced ones such as teamwork, influence skills, and managerial competence)(proficiency broadly), and more fundamental or advanced skills such as those of managing one's own learning, using higher-order thinking skills, and creativity in discerning and solving problems (proficiency in learning);
- broader talents such as personal and professional effectiveness and maturity (which outcomes may overlap or combine with knowledge and skills, but typically involve habit patterns, value commitments, and character structures).

Pascarella and Terenzini (1991) have presented a comprehensive examination of the various developmental aspects of education and methods of assessing outcomes in this area in *How College Affects Students.* They list, for example, greater complexity of thought as best differentiating seniors from entering students. Other listings abound. In all of them there is embedded the challenge for deciders (who should include the students themselves) to select and combine those target outcomes that will best serve the learners and society. Monitoring the degree of achievement of these outcomes is a task that is best provided by an academic administration that in turn will hold departments of instruction and individual instructors responsible for assessment.

Without effective monitoring to assure that implementation continues on track, a strategy for efficiency in learning can go far awry. Yet too much or too expensive a monitoring plan can also defeat the goal. Needed is an efficient, astutely designed system of assessment and feedback to guide the ongoing efforts to improve.

Very little energy and commitment have gone into the effort to document *efficiency in learning* as compared with that given to documenting costs and *cutting the costs of per credit produced.* (Teachers work at achieving learning efficiency a great deal, but much less at demonstrating it to others.) Often efforts focus on the "quality of instruction," not the actual learning outcomes, which are not shown to correlate highly with quality of instruction as measured.

In general, strategic plans of institutions of higher education do not include specific goals for effectiveness or efficiency in learning. Even widely heralded goals with supposed clarity may lack this specificity; (e.g., the commitment to improving critical thinking skills discussed in Chapter 6). Primary interest should not be in whether students can demonstrate these skills in a particular course, on a paper, or in an isolated exercise (i.e., they know *the content and* can use *the skill in the abstract*), but whether they can demonstrate critical thinking in the context of their jobs, their voting behaviors, and their daily lives. (Such assessment is sometimes called "authentic assessment.") Partnerships between colleges and employers on assessing performance of employer-supported students in the workplace could help answer this question.

The focus on outcomes works only if learning is measured in valid and reliable ways and if lessons learned are then used to redesign strategy or tactics to achieve the outcomes sought.

In a "meta-assessment" of 13 projects on student outcomes assessment conducted on eleven campuses of the California State University System, the key variable for all the successful projects was the development or adoption of adequate measures of student outcomes. The projects that successfully achieved student outcomes: (1) clearly defined goals; (2) selected outcomes related to the goals; and (3) developed measures of the outcomes (California State University, 1993).

Given well-chosen goals, a choice of learning outcomes suited to those goals, and valid and reliable ways of measuring achievement on those outcomes, what proportion of resources for facilitating students' learning may prudently be devoted to monitoring the institution's performance for the purpose of improving it? What, on the other hand, is a limit below which the investment in such monitoring should not sink? Precedents in higher education to guide decision on these questions are rare. The extent of monitoring needed doubtless varies with different situations, and astute timing (e.g., an early effort in setting expectations) can help. Yet in industry it would be considered unthinkable to make as low an investment in performance evaluation and product or service development as typifies American colleges today.

FOLLOW THE IMPLICATIONS OF THE INSTITUTION'S OVERALL STRATEGY IN DETAIL

There is good reason for pause about taking any model or scheme as generally applicable to the work of higher education. It is easier to declare a grand philosophy and to continue business as usual than to be faithful in every detail to the implications of a new learning framework such as that articulated on page 155 of this chapter. But if the framework is well chosen, being faithful to its implications in practice is a recipe for success. If the implications are not effective in practice, the framework is defective and should either be corrected or replaced. For example, early practice of simply transferring classroom practices to distance education on the Internet gave cause for reconsideration of that approach. The need for consistency between major strategies and minor ones goes beyond classroom and instructional practices. At a March 1995 conference on assessment at Educational Testing Service, Astin pointed out that the predominant use of outside assessment services by higher education up to now has been as a tool of selection, often of "selecting out" students. By contrast he urged a focus on talent development—that is, gains in learning and personal development by students. If we focus on talent development, the entering scores will be used not just to predict success rates but to establish expectancies and to encourage students with appropriate supports to exceed those expectations (Astin, 1998).

Colleges serving primarily adult students often dispense with admissions testing altogether, overlooking the potential of assessment at entry for intelligent planning of students, choices of courses and of the supports they may need for optimal development of their talents. In defense of this omission, authorities argue that no appropriate measures of potential for college studies are available for adults who are more than five years out of high school. If so, a key implication of the efficiency in learning strategy for those students is missing.

We conclude this book with one further element of sound management: a sensible division of labor in governance and management.

LET ROLES IN ACCOUNTABILITY FIT THE GRAND STRATEGY

In one of America's most competitive types of enterprise, professional football, it is widely appreciated that, while owners have a right and a duty to choose the coaches and approve the budget, having the owner call the plays would be a recipe for disaster. Fans are, of course, indispensable to the economy of the trade; but even their Monday-morning calls would not work out well over the season. The art of finding and enlisting the right chief executives and of their engaging, in turn, the ablest administrators is one that has its own extensive literature. What may need saying here is a few words about where accountability for a college or university's performance should rest.

The pursuit of efficiency in learning at postsecondary level is a highly complex undertaking that requires the full attention and energies of a competent managerial team. The most significant improvements may be expected from more astute choices of overall strategy, as illustrated on pages 148-157 of this chapter. A second and equally significant set of improvements could come from changes in the practice of teaching and learning, which we addressed in Chapters 1 through 7. Much less likely to help are interventions in specific administrative and teaching practice by legislative, accrediting, and trustee bodies. Their roles differ, but include those of demanding appropriate accountability, choosing and appointing the executives, and insisting on the appropriate efficiencies. Like owners and fans second guessing head professional football coaches, it is unlikely that supervisory authorities will do better by direct intervention in running the institutions' operations.

Within a few decades university students may have a hard time imagining a university faculty staffed with teachers overwhelmingly of one ethnic background or of only a few of the planet's national cultures. Throughout history academies of high repute were distinguished by an outstanding faculty, a large library, and excellent classroom and laboratory facilities. In contrast, the key characteristics of the model university of the 21st century are likely to be an ethnically and culturally diverse faculty, a state-of-the-art information-retrieval and processing system, provision for asynchronous and global access to outstanding faculty and facilities by students, and a system for integrated support for individualized learning and development agendas of its ethnically and culturally diverse students. Institutions of higher education, possibly focused on special student populations or special curricular purposes, will nevertheless be obliged to select and build their resources of people, facilities, and equipment to take advantage of the rapid changes in the means of learning afforded by the economies and technology of the future.

REFERENCES

Aslanian, D. B. & Brickell, H. M. (1980). *Americans in transition.* New York: College Entrance Examination Board.

Astin, A. (1998). Assessment, student development, and public policy. In Messick, S. J. (Ed.), *Assessment in higher education* (chapter 13). Mahwah, N. J.: Erlbaum Associates.

Barrows, H. S. (1994). *Practice-based learning: Problem-based learning applied to medical education.* Springfield, IL: Southern Illinois University School of Medicine.

Blanco, C. D. (1994). *Doing more with less: Approaches to shortening time to degree.* Denver: State Higher Education Executive Officers (SHEEO). November.

Bowne, P. & Engelmann, D. (1999). Improving Effectiveness and Efficiency in Teaching and Learning for Intermediate Students (Alverno College). In M. T. Keeton (Ed.): *Effectiveness and Efficiency in Learning: Case Studies.* Adelphi, MD: Institute for Research on Adults in Higher Education

California State University (1993). *Academic challenges: Student outcomes assessment.* Long Beach, CA: California State University, Office of the Chancellor. [ERIC ED 363225].

Dey, E. & Hurtado, S. (1994). Latino student transition to college: Assessing difficulties and factors in successful college adjustment (Number #D373663). Paper presented at the Annual Forum of the Association for Institutional Research (1993). University of Michigan, Ann Arbor: Center for the Study of Higher and Postsecondary Education.

Eaton, J. S. (1991). *The unfinished agenda: Higher education and the 1980s.* New York, NY: American Council on Education, Macmillan Publishing Company.

Hollins, C. S. (Ed.) (1992, Fall). Containing costs and improving productivity in higher education. *New Directions for Institutional Research, 75.* San Francisco: Jossey-Bass.

Hudgins, J. L. (1993). Institutional effectiveness: A maturing movement. Where do we go from here? Paper presented at the Summer Institute of the Community College Consortium, Madison, WI. [ERIC ED358891]

Johnstone, D. B. (1993). College at work: The new imperative for American higher education. *Educational Record,* 49-52.

Keeton, M. (1999a). Cooperative Education at Antioch College. In M. T. Keeton (Ed.): *Effectiveness and Efficiency in Learning: Case Studies.* Adelphi, MD: Institute for Research on Adults in Higher Education

Keeton, M. (1999b). Individualized Degree Programs for Adults: Empire State College. In M. T. Keeton (Ed.): *Effectiveness and Efficiency in Learning: Case Studies.* Adelphi: MD. Institute for Research on Adults in Higher Education.

Kehrhahn, M., Sheckley, B. G., & Travers, N. L. (2000). *Efficiency and effectiveness in graduate education: A case analysis.* (Vol. 76): Association for Institutional Research.

Koschmann, T., Kelson, A. C., Feltovich, P. J., & Barrows, H. S. (1996). Computer-supported problem-based learning: A principled approach to the use of computers in collaborative learning. In T. Koschmann (Ed.): *CSCL: Theory and practice of an emerging paradigm.* Mahwah, NJ: Lawrence Erlbaum Associates.

Kotler, P. & Stonich, P. J. (1991, September/October). Turbo marketing through time compression, *The Journal of Business Strategy,* 24-29.

Kraft, R. J. (1995). A summary of the educational reform reports. In R. J. Kraft & J. Kielmeier (Eds.): *Experiential learning in schools and higher education.* Dubuque: Kendall/Hunt Publishing Company.

Mathews, J. (1995, April 1). Stretching out classes to suit students' pace: Going slower may be fastest way to learn. *The Washington Post,* p. A3.

Mente, S. (1999). Course Innovations in Developmental Math (Alverno College). In M. T. Keeton (Ed.): *Effectiveness and Efficiency in Learning: Case Studies.* Adelphi, MD: Institute for Research on Adults in Higher Education

Pascarella, E. T. & Terenzini, P. T. (1991). *How colleges affect students.* San Francisco: Jossey-Bass.

Porosky, J. (1999) Keys to Efficiency at University of Maryland University College. In M. T. Keeton (Ed.): *Effectiveness and Efficiency in Learning: Case Studies.* Adelphi: MD. Institute for Research on Adults in Higher Education.

Prather, G. (1993, November). The who, whom, and how of institutional accountability. Paper presented at the annual Convention of the Community College League of California, Burlingame. [ERIC 366377].

Tinto, V. (1987). *Leaving college: Rethinking the causes and cures of student attrition.* Chicago: University of Chicago Press.

Twigg, C.A. & Doucette, D. (1992). *Leadership abstracts, 5* (6). Laguna Hills, CA: League for Innovation in the Community College and the Community College Leadership Program.

Wilcox, F. K. (1999) Supplemental Instruction: Review of Research Concerning the Effectiveness of SI from the University of Missouri-Kansas City and Other Institutions from Across the United States. In M. T. Keeton (Ed.): *Effectiveness and Efficiency in Learning: Case Studies.* Adelphi: MD: Institute for Research on Adults in Higher Education.

Wilson, J. M. (1994). The CUPLE physics studio. *The Physics Teacher, 32:* (9) 18-523.

Wisan, G. (1999). Current Student Survey, Report of the Office of Accountability, Institutional Planning, and Assessment. Adelphi, MD: University of Maryland University College.

Witkowski, S. & Magness, D. (1999). Integrated Language Practice: Efficiency and Effectiveness in Learning (Alverno College). In M. T. Keeton (Ed.): *Effectiveness and Efficiency in Learning: Case Studies.* Adelphi, MD: Institute for Research on Adults in Higher Education.

APPENDIX A
Inventory of Cited Cases of Efficient Practice from IRAHE 's Practitioners' Handbook

These studies, initially reported as indicated below, have been excerpted and further edited by Morris Keeton for use in this book. All are saved in a file entitled M. T. Keeton: *Effectiveness and Efficiency in Learning: Case Studies.* Adelphi, MD: Institute for Research on Adults in Higher Education. University of Maryland University College.

1. Mente, S. (1994). Course Innovations in Developmental Math (Alverno College)
2. Bowne, P. & Engelmann, D. (1993). Improving Effectiveness and Efficiency in Teaching and Learning for Intermediate Students (Alverno College)
3. Witkowski, S. & Magness, D. (1993). Integrated Language Practice: Efficiency and Effectiveness in Learning (Alverno College)
4. Keeton, M. (1999). Cooperative Education at Antioch College.
5. Keeton, M. (1999). Individualized Degree Programs for Adults: Empire State College
6. Shaffmaster, L. & Langan, F. G. (1993) The Early Childhood Education Professional Preparation Project: A Case Study in Adult Learning (Keystone Junior College)
7. Clagett, C. A. & Engleberg, I. N. (1998) The R-Cubed Academy at Prince George's Community College (MD)
8. Peinovich, P. (1993) Degree Completion Through Collaboration: A Case for Efficiency
9. Kehrhahn, M., Cordeira, P. & Sheckley, B. G. (1993) Efficiency in Doctoral Studies (University of Connecticut) (Later revised and published in the AIR Professional File.)
10. Stupka, E. (1993) Right to Succeed Courses (Sacramento City College)
11. Schreck, R. (1993) Internships in Business for Students of Irkutsk State University
12. Porosky, J. (1993) Keys to Efficiency at University of Maryland University College (UMUC)

13. Janke, T. & Myers, A. (1993) Cost Effectiveness in a UMUC Nuclear Science Program
14. Hoffman, T., Legrow, M. & Sheckley, B. G. (1999) Making Prior Learning Assessment Pay Its Way: Three Case Studies (written by Morris Keeton on the basis of two earlier case studies by Hoffmann and a third by LeGrow et al. (In the text of this book we cite an extended article by Legrow.)
15. Wilcox, F. K. (1993) Supplemental Instruction: Review of Research Concerning the Effectiveness of SI from the University of Missouri-Kansas City and Other Institutions from Across the United States
16. Millar, S. (1993) The "Learning through Evaluation, Assessment, and Dissemination/Engagement" (LEAD) Project in the University of Wisconsin-Madison Emerging Scholars Program

NOTE: There are numerous additional case studies that were funded by IRAHE but that are not cited in this book as well as other published case studies that ARE cited in the book, but that did not have IRAHE funding.